C000226950

weimaran

understanding and
caring for your breed

Written by
Alice Thornton

weimaraner

understanding and
caring for your breed

Written by
Alice Thornton

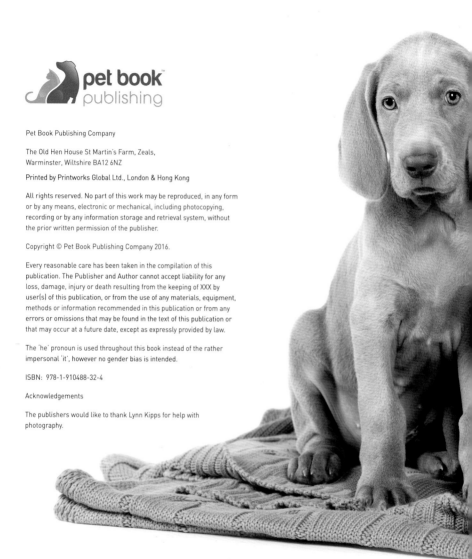

Pet Book Publishing Company

The Old Hen House St Martin's Farm, Zeals,
Warminster, Wiltshire BA12 6NZ

Printed by Printworks Global Ltd., London & Hong Kong

ISBN: 978-1-910488-32-4

Acknowledgements

The publishers would like to thank Lynn Kipps for help with
photography.

Contents

Introducing the Weimaraner

The Weimaraner, with his unique grey coat and bewitching amber eyes, is known as the ghost dog. This conjures up an air of mystery but, in many ways, the Weimaraner is an open book. Loving and affectionate, this lively and intelligent dog is the perfect companion for an active family.

Physical characteristics

The Weimaraner is a member of the hunt, point, retrieve (HPR) group of gundogs which were developed in Europe. These supremely talented breeds, which include the German Shorthaired Pointer, the Hungarian Vizsla and the Italian Spinone – are designed to perform all the tasks on the hunting field, rather than specialising in a specific role in the way of Spaniels, Retrievers, Pointers and Setters. As a gundog that was required

to work all day in the field, the Weimaraner needed the physical capabilities to carry out the strenuous work of hunting, pointing and retrieving. Power, speed, stamina – and terrific scenting powers – were essential to track, mark and retrieve game. He also needed a strong neck and a soft mouth to enable him to pick it up. Taking all this into consideration, the Weimaraner is a picture of grace and balance; he has a muscular build but he is well proportioned which gives him an air of clean-cut elegance. He has strong, straight forelegs, a deep chest, a level back and angulated hindquarters.

Traditionally, a working gundog had a cropped tail to prevent injury when working in undergrowth but companion dogs in most countries, with the exception of the USA, now have full tails. The Weimaraner has a refined, aristocratic head framed by long ears which are folded and set on high. As scenting is of paramount importance he has a large nose with well-developed nostrils.

The medium-sized eyes, set well apart are a feature of the breed. They come in shades of amber – the traditional ghost dog colour – or shades of blue grey. Puppies have sky blue eyes, which are highly arresting.

In order to work in all weathers, often retrieving from water, the Weimaraner needed a weatherproof

Other Hunt, Point, Retrieve Breeds

Hungarian Vizsla

Italian Spinone

German Shorthaired Pointer

coat. There are two varieties: the smooth, sleek coat of the short-haired Weimaraner and the long-coated variety which is not seen so often.

The Weimaraner has a stunning coat colour – a beautiful silver grey, with the appearance of metallic sheen.

Temperament

A gundog works closely with his handler, and there are also times when he needs to take the initiative. The Weimaraner is a sound worker and is always biddable, but there are some interesting facets to his character.

The Breed Standard, which is the written blueprint for the breed, picks out the following adjectives to describe him:

Fearless: Bred originally to hunt large game – boar, bear and deer – the Weimaraner needs the courage to hold his ground.

Friendly: This is an endearing trait shared by the gundog breeds. The Weimaraner loves people and enjoys interacting with them.

Protective: The Weimaraner has the instinctive ability to guard, but this is not necessarily a virtue in a companion dog.

A Weimaraner may be keen to protect his home and family but this behaviour should be kept in check so that it does not become problematical.

Obedient: A readiness to co-operate is essential in a working dog, and it is very useful in a companion dog, too!

Alert: A hunting dog needs to be alive to changing situations; the intelligent Weimaraner is constantly checking on what is going on around him

Easy-going: This is typified in the Weimaraner's adaptable nature.

Here we have a picture of an intelligent, versatile dog that bonds closely with his human family.

He has a bold, enthusiastic outlook on life but he is also a thinking dog which means he can be determined in some aspects of his behaviour and stubborn in others. He needs to be trained with tact and understanding to bring out the best in him.

The ideal home

The Weimaraner is described as being medium-sized but this is an agile, energetic breed so you get a lot of dog for your money.

For this reason, a Weimaraner is better suited to country life where there are more opportunities for the extensive exercise he needs. However, the Weimaraner is adaptable and if you can provide an outlet for his abundant energy he will fit in with an urban lifestyle.

This is a breed that gets on well with children, and thrives on the hurly burly of family life. He needs mental stimulation as well as physical exercise, and he will be delighted if you want to get involved in one of the canine sports.

He is still prized as a consummate hunting dog, carrying out his hunt, point, retrieve activities with great flair, but there is no doubt that his primary role is as a wonderful companion dog.

He relishes the love and affection he is given by all members of his human family, and in return he gives his unstinting loyalty.

Facing page: An active home, with plenty of mental stimulation, is a must for the Weimaraner.

Tracing back in time

The Weimaraner's recent history is easy to trace as the breed was named after the city of Weimar, now in the province of Thuringa in modern-day Germany. But what are the origins of these distinctive looking hunting dogs?

It is well documented that the Weimaraner was developed as a hunting dog by Grand Duke Karl August around 1775. At that time the aristocracy were preoccupied with tracking and hunting boar, bear and deer, and they needed a fast athletic dog with the courage and tenacity to pursue and mark prey of this size.

They therefore worked with the hunting dogs that best suited their purpose and then refined them into a breed in its own right.

French connections

In the 14th century, at the court of Louis IX in France, there was a pack of large, grey hunting dogs which were known as the Chien Gris de Saint Louis.

These dogs, which are thought to have come from Egypt, were highly valued for their working ability and were given as gifts to courts in neighbouring European countries. There were three types of hunting dog in use:

Alaunt: A fierce dog, with great speed, that could bring down large prey.

Levrier: Resembling a modern-day Greyhound, this dog hunted by sight.

Courant: Hunting by scent, this dog had a broad muzzle and long, pendulous ears.

The Chien Gris de Saint Louis was considered to be the elite of the Courant hunting dogs, and they were given the very special privilege of living in the homes of their handlers. Their popularity was uncontested for the next two centuries; they were featured in many paintings and tapestries proving their status as supreme hunting dog.

In the 1700s, white hunting dogs came into fashion but the Chien Gris de Saint Louis was still very much in evidence. However, the introduction of firearms in the early 19th century had a major impact on every aspect of hunting throughout Europe. Hunting birds was preferred over big game, and this required a lighter-built dog that could quarter the ground and hold quarry on point.

In the UK, breeders strived to create specialist

hunting dogs, whereas in Europe there was a preference for maintaining a gundog that was capable of carrying out all the tasks – hunting, pointing and retrieving – that were required in the field.

Creating the Weimaraner

In the city of Weimar, Grand Duke Karl August became active in creating a new breed that would be the perfect all-rounder. The Chien Gris de Saint Louis provided the foundation for his breeding stock, and new lines were added to improve conformation and working ability.

There is much speculation as to the breeds that were used to create the Weimaraner; the Pointer, the Spanish Pointer, the German Shorthaired Pointer, the Great Dane, the Saint Hubertus Bracke, the Bloodhound and the Schweisshund have all been named.

Unfortunately, there is no concrete evidence as the Grand Duke Karl August ruled his court with an iron fist. He held the veto on who could own a Weimaraner, and he was highly secretive about his dogs and their breeding.

All written records have been lost or destroyed – maybe to maintain the breed's mystery.

The Weimaraner's hunting ability was enhanced by introducing breeds such as the Bloodhound into his genetic make up.

Developing the breed

In 1880 the German Delegate Commission received a request for the Weimaraner to be recognised as a breed in its own right. Initially, this met with strong opposition as purists claimed that the grey all-round hunting dog was a German Shorthaired Pointer in a different colour...

Behind the scenes, enthusiasts for the new breed were hard at work; they drew up a Breed Standard in 1894 and campaigned vigorously until official recognition was gained the following year.

The first breed club was founded in 1897 and its name – the Club for Pure Breeding of Silver Grey Weimaraner Pointers – indicates the struggle for identity. The club was later renamed the German Weimaraner Club.

The war years

The versatile Weimaraner prospered on the shooting field and became the breed of choice for many. However, the First World War (1914-1918) had a devastating effect on the breed and by the end of it there were barely a dozen Weimaraners left in Germany.

Dedicated breeders resurrected the breed, ensuring that, despite the scarcity of stock, only the best dogs were selected for breeding. Major Robert aus der Herber, president of the German Weimaraner Club from 1921-1946, was a leading light and the club's aims were summed up by its motto: "It is not the breed, but the breeder's selection that guarantees highest quality of conformation and best performance." The Weimaraner started to become established outside Germany – the first pair of Weimaraners reached America in 1929 and sportsmen were swift to appreciate the breed's prowess on the hunting field. The versatile Weimaraner was now the perfect choice for hunting small game; an expert birder and with a terrific nose for rabbit, hare and fox.

The outbreak of the Second World War in 1939 put an end to breeding, hunting and showing activities In Europe. This time there was no immediate resurgence; the peace terms imposed on Germany by the allied forces put a ban on firearms, showing and hunting. It was not until 1951 that the restrictions were lifted and the German Weimaraner Club could be reformed.

Post war years

Despite the hardships and restrictions of the war years, the Weimaraner's reputation grew rapidly as the occupying forces discovered the breed and started exporting dogs to the UK, to the USA and to neighbouring European countries. In fact, the demand for Weimaraners was so great the German Weimaraner Club imposed a rule that only half of each new litter could be exported. This allowed sufficient scope for the breed to re-establish itself in its native home.

There was strong American interest in the Weimaraner prior to the Second World War; in 1943 the Weimaraner Club of America was established and breeding and showing continued throughout the war years.

In the 1950s the breed went from strength to strength with imports of top-quality dogs from Germany; it was not long before breeders established their own gene pool and were exporting dogs to the UK.

The first Weimaraners reached the UK in 1952. While in the army, Major R.H. Petty (later known for his Strawbridge kennel) and Major Eric Richardson (who bred using the Monksway affix) discovered the Weimaraner and imported Cobra von Boberstrand and Bando von Fohr.

In the same year, an in-whelp bitch was imported from the USA and her son, Thunderjet, was the Best Dog at Crufts in 1955. The Weimaraner had arrived in style!

The Weimaraner today

The Weimaraner has a relatively short history outside its native home but the breed has now spread worldwide, mostly relying on American bloodlines.

The Weimaraner is still highly valued as a hunting dog and even though he is becoming increasingly popular as a show dog, he retains the conformation and temperament of his working forebears.

Stunning to look at, athletic and intelligent, the Weimaraner will make his mark in all the canine sports. But – perhaps most importantly of all – the Weimaraner is a loyal and loving dog and will be a devoted family companion.

The long-haired Weimaraner

The first long-haired Weimaraner was exhibited at the Hanover show in 1879. But the first long-haired to receive official recognition was a dog called Tell von Stanzendorf, whelped in Austria in 1933, the offspring of short-haired parents.

Despite assurances by the breeder, Josef Schaffer, that the pup would lose his "fluffy coat," he grew into a handsome, long-haired adult. The dog, proudly owned by Robert Pattay, was first shown in Vienna in 1934.

Major Herber, an authority on the breed, researched Tell von Stanzendorf's bloodlines and he came to the conclusion that the long coat was a natural variant. Following lengthy discussions, the long-haired Weimaraner gained official recognition in 1935.

What should a Weimaraner look like?

The Weimaraner, with his athletic build and stunning coat colour, stands out in any crowd. So what should the perfect Weimaraner look like?

The aim of breeders is to produce dogs that are sound, healthy, typical examples of their chosen breed, in terms of both looks and temperament.

To achieve this, they are guided by a Breed Standard, which is a written blueprint describing the perfect specimen.

Of course, there is no such thing as a 'perfect' dog, but breeders aspire to produce dogs that conform as closely as possible to the picture in words presented by the Breed Standard. In the show ring, judges use

the Breed Standard to assess the dogs that come before them, and it is the dog that, in their opinion, comes closest to the ideal, that will win top honours.

This has significance beyond the sport of showing, for it is the dogs that win in the ring which will be used for breeding. The winners of today are therefore responsible for passing on their genes to future generations and preserving the breed in its best form.

There are some differences in the wording of the Breed Standard depending on national kennel clubs; the American Kennel Club and the Federation Cynologique Internationale, which is the governing body for 86 countries, have far more descriptive Standards than the brief outline given in the English version.

General appearance

The Weimaraner is a versatile all-round gundog, and his ability to work in the field is of paramount importance, governing the way he looks and moves. He presents a picture of power and speed but with the stamina and endurance to keep going all day.

His conformation is balanced and although he is strong and muscular, a mature Weimaraner also appears graceful and elegant.

Temperament

The FCI Breed Standard describes the Weimaraner as being easy-going but this is deceptive. He is easy to live with as long as you understand him. This is a dog with strong mental powers and although he is friendly and biddable, he is fearless in outlook and has a strong protective streak.

Head

The Weimaraner's head is described as being aristocratic. The skull is broad and domed; the stop (the step-up between the muzzle and forehead) is moderate. The measurement from the top of the nose to the stop should equal the measurement from the stop to the occiput (the bony prominence at the back of the skull).

The flews (lips) are moderately deep, enclosing powerful jaws. The foreface is straight and the nose, which is grey in colour, has well-developed nostrils. The skin is tightly drawn over the head, with no wrinkle. Male and female can be recognised by head shape; the male's head is larger and broader but it should not be coarse.

Eyes

The Weimaraner's eye colour is a feature of the breed. A youngster has piercing blue eyes which change to amber in maturity. The shade of amber ranges from dark to light and includes a blue/grey colour. The medium sized eyes are placed far apart, indicating a good disposition; the expression is keen and intelligent but with unmistakable kindness.

Ears

The ears are set on high and hang downwards, with a slight fold.

The British Standard states that when the ear is drawn alongside the muzzle, it should finish approximately 2.5cm (1in) from the point of the nose, whereas the American Standard stipulates a measurement of 5cm (2in) from the nose.

The FCI does not give a precise measurement, confining itself to stating that the ear should reach to "about the corner of the mouth". In fact, the fold of the ear, noticeable when a dog is alert, is more important as it contributes to the typical Weimaraner expression.

Mouth

The Weimaraner has powerful jaws which meet in a perfect scissor bite with the teeth on the upper jaw closely overlapping the teeth on the lower jaw. The teeth should be strong, even and well set; the lips and gums are flesh coloured.

Neck

The neck is muscular, clean cut and moderately long; it is an important feature as it supports the dog when he is carrying heavy game, sometimes over rough and uneven terrain. The FCI gives a more detailed description stating that the neck should be of "noble and stately appearance". Most importantly, it should merge harmoniously into the backline and chest.

Points of anatomy

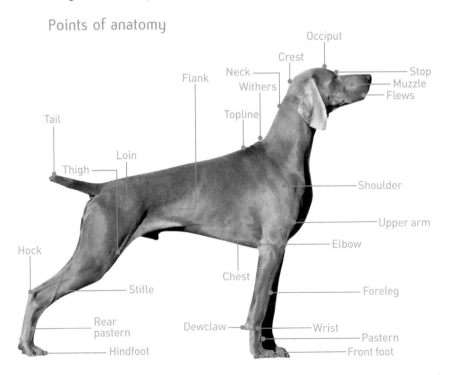

Occiput
Crest
Neck
Flank
Withers
Stop
Muzzle
Flews
Topline
Tail
Loin
Thigh
Shoulder
Upper arm
Elbow
Hock
Chest
Stifle
Foreleg
Rear pastern
Dewclaw
Wrist
Hindfoot
Pastern
Front foot

Forequarters

The forelegs are straight and strong; the measurement from the elbow to the ground should equal the distance from the elbow to the top of the withers (the highest point of the shoulder). They should not be too close together as the Weimaraner needs chest room. The shoulders are long and sloping with a good length of upper arm; correct construction is needed to carry the weight of the forequarters.

Body

The topline is level, with a slightly sloping croup (muscular area at the dog's rump). The chest is well developed and the shoulders are well laid. The chest is powerful but it should not be too wide; the ideal depth of chest nearly reaches the elbows. This is a dog that is built for speed, stamina and endurance so he needs well-sprung ribs and his ribcage extends well back.

Hindquarters

The hindquarters are muscular and moderately angulated, according to the British Standard, and well angulated, according to the American Standard. The stifle (knee) is well turned and the hocks (ankles) are well let down, turning neither in nor out.

In terms of overall balance, the angulation of the stifle should be in harmony with the angulation of the shoulder.

Feet

The feet are firm and compact with well-arched toes. The pads are close and thick providing a cushion for the dog when he is working over rough terrain. The nails are grey or amber in colour.

Tail

The tail was customarily docked to a length where it covered the scrotum in males and the vulva in females. This gave sufficient length for the dog to change the carriage and express his feelings, as well as being visible when working in long grass and undergrowth.

Working gundogs may still have their tails docked and in the USA docking is permitted regardless of the dog's status. However in the UK, and in most other parts of the world, docking is illegal for pet dogs.

The full tail should reach down to the hocks and taper towards the tip. It is carried below the level of the back when the dog is relaxed but it may be raised when he is animated. The tail should never curl over the back.

Coat

The short-haired Weimaraner's coat is smooth and sleek. The long-haired Weimaraner has a coat that is roughly 2.5-5cm (1-2in) long on the body; it is longer on the neck, chest and belly with feathering on the tail and the back of the legs.

Colour

The Weimaraner boasts a unique coat colour; it is preferably silver grey but all shades from mouse grey to silver grey are acceptable. The colour may be lighter on the head and ears. Quite often, a Weimaraner will have a dark eel stripe along the length of his back. A small white mark is permissible on the chest.

Movement

In order to work, the Weimaraner needs an effortless, ground-covering stride, indicating smooth co-ordination. When viewed from behind, the hind legs should be parallel to the front feet. When looking from the side, the topline should remain strong and level.

Size

There is a slight difference in size requirements depending on the Breed Standard. The British

Standard asks for males to be 61-69cm (24-27in) at the withers, females should be 56-64cm (22-25in). The American Standard has a narrower margin: males 64-69cm (25-27in), females 58-64cm (23-25in). It states that one inch variation on either side of the specified heights is allowable but if this is exceeded the dog would be disqualified from the show ring.

Good looks aside, the Weimaraner must always be fit for function.

Summing up

Although the majority of Weimaraners are kept as pet dogs and will never be exhibited in the show ring, it is important that breeders strive for perfection and try to produce dogs that adhere as closely as possible to the Breed Standard. This is the best way of ensuring that the Weimaraner remains sound in mind and body, and retains the characteristics that are unique to this very special breed.

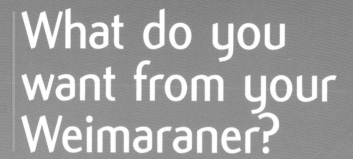

What do you want from your Weimaraner?

There are over 200 dog breeds to choose from, so how can you be sure that the Weimaraner is the right breed for you? Before you decide on a Weimaraner you need to be 100 per cent confident that this is the breed that is best suited to your lifestyle.

Companion

Loving and loyal, the Weimaraner has adapted perfectly to the role of companion dog. He is an active, energetic dog and loves to be involved in all family activities.

If you have a family with small children, the Weimaraner will be an ideal playmate, as long as you establish the ground rules on both sides. A Weimaraner can be boisterous, particularly when he is growing up, so you need to teach self-control when he is around children.

As far as the children are concerned, they need to understand that a dog needs some quiet times when he is not disturbed, such as when he is eating or sleeping.

He is not a toy to be poked and prodded at will. If these rules are followed and mutual respect is established, a Weimaraner will become an integral member of the family circle. The Weimaraner does need extensive exercise so he may not be a good choice for those who are frail or getting on in years.

Working dog

If you interested in owning a working gundog, a Weimaraner could well be the breed for you. This versatile, hunt, point, retrieve breed is expert at scenting game, holding it on point and then bringing it to hand. He has the intelligence to work on his own initiative and the stamina to work from dawn to dusk.

Sports dog

The adaptable Weimaraner has proved his worth in all the canine sports, ranging from field trials, where he can show off his inherited hunting skills, to obedience and agility where he works closely with his handler. For more information, see Opportunities for Weimaraners.

Show dog

Do you have ambitions to exhibit your Weimaraner in the show ring? This is a highly competitive sport, with big entries in all the classes, so you do need the right dog to begin with.

If you plan to show your Weimaraner you need to track down a show quality puppy, and train him so he will perform in the ring, and accept the detailed 'hands on' examination which is part of the judging process. It is also important to bear in mind that not every puppy with show potential develops into a top quality specimen, and so you must be prepared to love your Weimaraner and give him a home for life, even if he doesn't make the grade.

What does your Weimaraner want from you?

A dog cannot speak for himself, so we need to view the world from a canine perspective and work out what a Weimaraner needs in order to live a happy, contented and fulfilling life.

Time and commitment

First of all, a Weimaraner needs a commitment that you will care for him for the duration of his life, guiding him through his puppyhood, enjoying his adulthood, and being there for him in his later years. If all potential owners were prepared to make this pledge, there would be scarcely any dogs in rescue.

The Weimaraner is a superb companion dog, but he does not come ready-made. You need to take charge

of his education, guiding him through puppyhood and adolescence, so that he understands his place in the family. His considerable brain needs to be occupied; a bored Weimaraner will be quick to find his own agenda, so you need to find the time to provide mental stimulation.

You also need to bear in mind that a Weimaraner needs to be a fully fledged member of the family. If he is excluded from family activities or expected to spend lengthy periods on his own, he will not only be thoroughly miserable, but he may well invent his own agenda and spend the time barking and whining or being destructive.

It is important that all dogs can cope with spending some time on their own so they don't become anxious, but the maximum time a dog should be left is four hours.

If this does not fit in with your lifestyle, you should delay owning a dog until your circumstances change.

Practical matters

The Weimaraner is a relatively low maintenance dog when it comes to looking after him. In terms of coat care, the short-haired Weimaraner needs minimal grooming and although long-haired dogs need more care, a regular routine of bushing and combing is all that is required. Exercise is essential for this sporting dog – and that means in all weathers! A Weimaraner thrives in an active home and dog walking should be a pleasure for all concerned.

Leadership

The Weimaraner is not a challenging breed – as long as you get his measure. This is a highly intelligent dog that has a mind of his own. He is obedient and biddable, but he needs a leader he respects.

It is your job to show your Weimaraner how you want him to behave by rewarding the behaviour that you consider desirable.

You need to be 100 per cent consistent, so he is left in no doubt as to what is deemed acceptable. If he pushes the boundaries or misbehaves, interrupt his undesirable behaviour by ignoring him or refocusing his attention.

As soon as he makes the 'right' decision and changes his behaviour, you can reward him handsomely. In this way, your Weimaraner learns good manners without the need for force or coercion. He is living with you in peace and harmony because he respects you.

Teenage tantrums

The Weimaraner has a stubborn streak and there may be occasions when he digs in his heels and refuses to co-operate with you. This is most likely to happen during adolescence and females are more prone to this type of behaviour than males.

If your Weimaraner throws a tantrum, do not be alarmed. It is a passing phase and, if handled correctly, will soon disappear. The key is to be non-confrontational as starting a battle of wills will only exacerbate the situation. Try to distract him by asking him to do something straightforward, such as a sit or a down, so you can reward him with a treat or a toy, thus changing his mindset from opposition to co-operation.

If he is not responding, put him in his crate for a short cooling off period. This is not a punishment, and you must make quite sure that you do not reprimand him or drag him by the collar. Simply put him in his crate and give him some space.

This effectively diffuses the situation so when you go and get him you can start again with a clean slate. Now ask him to do something easy so you can reward him, thus re-estabishing a relationship that is based on positives.

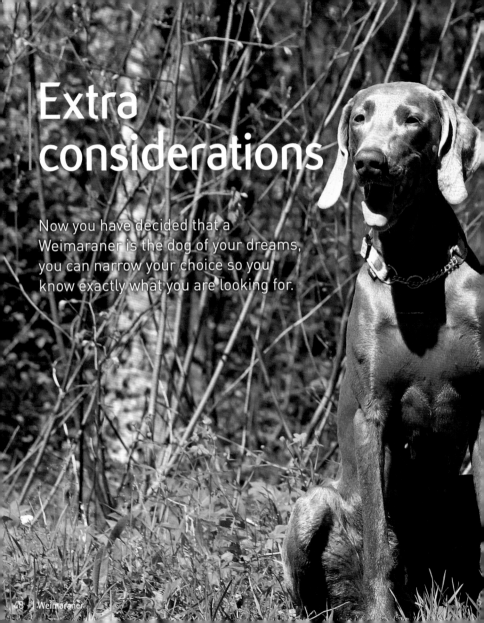

Extra considerations

Now you have decided that a Weimaraner is the dog of your dreams, you can narrow your choice so you know exactly what you are looking for.

Male or female?

The choice of male or female Weimaraner comes down to personal preference. Males are bigger than females – and this does not just refer to their height.

A male is a more substantial animal with considerably more power and strength. This will be particularly noticeable during adolescence when dogs tend to be boisterous and lack self-control.

In terms of temperament, both male and female are loyal and loving. It is probably true to say that a female can be more manipulative, and she can be aloof at times. A male is generally more even-tempered, and some owners report that male dogs are especially patient with children.

If you opt for a female, you will need to cope with her seasons, which will start at around 12 months of age and occur approximately every nine months thereafter.

During the three-week period of a season, you will need to keep your bitch away from entire males (males that have not been neutered) to eliminate the risk of an unwanted pregnancy. Some owners also report that females may be a little moody and withdrawn during their seasonal cycle.

Many pet owners opt for neutering, which puts an

end to the seasons, and also has many attendant health benefits. The operation, known as spaying, is usually carried out at some point after the first season. The best plan is to seek advice from your vet.

An entire male may not cause many problems, although some do have a stronger tendency to mark, which could include inside the house. However, training will usually put a stop to this. An entire male will also be on the lookout for bitches in season, and this may lead to difficulties, depending on your circumstances. Neutering (castrating) a male is a relatively simple operation, and there are associated health benefits. Again, you should seek advice from your vet.

Coat type

The short-haired Weimaraner is the more popular of the two varieties, and there is no doubt that a close-fitting coat enhances the breed's athletic lines.

Obviously there is more work involved in keeping a long-haired Weimaraner in good order but the coat is not excessive. There is a view that the long-haired Weimaraner has a slightly different temperament and in terms of working ability he is more 'birdy', meaning he is preoccupied with watching and air-scenting birds.

More than one?

Owning a Weimaraner can be addictive and you may want to expand your canine population. However, think carefully before you go ahead. A Weimaraner needs training and leadership and you need to have the time to interact with each dog individually as well as doing things together.

Be wary of a breeder who encourages you to buy two puppies from the same litter, as it is unlikely that the welfare of the puppies is their top priority.

Pups of the same or similar ages will bond with each other rather than with you – and they will get up to all sorts of mischief. Most responsible breeders have a waiting list of potential purchasers before a litter is even born and have no need to make this type of sale.

If you do decide to take on a second Weimaraner, wait at least 18 months so your first dog is fully trained and settled before embarking on a puppy.

In terms of gender, it is best to avoid getting two males as they may vie with each other for top dog status. Females are more peaceable but a male/ female combination is probably the best option. If you go ahead with this, obviously one or both dogs will need to be neutered.

An older dog

You may decide to miss out on the puppy phase and take on an older dog instead. Such a dog may be harder to track down, but sometimes a breeder may have a youngster that is not suitable for showing, but is perfect for a family pet. In some cases, a breeder may rehome a female when her breeding career is at an end so she will enjoy the benefits of more individual attention.

There are advantages to taking on an older dog, as you know exactly what you are getting.

But the upheaval of changing homes can be quite upsetting for an older dog, so you will need to have plenty of patience during the settling in period.

Two Weimaraners of a similar age will be more than double the trouble...

Rehoming a rescued dog

We are fortunate that the number of Weimaraners that end up in rescue is relatively small. However, there are a number of dogs that need rehoming through no fault of their own.

The reasons are various, ranging from illness or death of the original owner to family breakdown, changing jobs, or even the arrival of a new baby.

You are unlikely to find a Weimaraner in an all-breed rescue centre; contacting a specialist breed club that runs a rescue scheme will be your best option if you decide to go down this route.

Try to find out as much as you can about a dog's history so you know exactly what you are taking on. You need to be aware of age and health status, likes and dislikes, plus any behavioural issues that may be relevant. You need to be realistic about what you are capable of achieving so you can be sure you can give the dog in question a permanent home.

Regardless of the dog's previous history, you will need to give him plenty of time and be patient with him as he settles into his new home. It may take weeks, or even months before he becomes fully integrated in the family, but if all goes well you will have the reward of knowing that you have given a Weimaraner a second chance.

Facing page: Can you give a Weimaraner a second chance of finding a forever home?

Sourcing a puppy

Your aim is to find a healthy puppy that is typical of the breed, and has been reared with the greatest possible care. Where do you start?

A tried and trusted method of finding a puppy is to attend a dog show where your chosen breed is being exhibited. This will give you the opportunity to see lots of different Weimaraners of all ages.

To begin with they may look very much the same, but when you look closely you will detect that there are different 'types' on show.

They are all pure-bred Weimaraners, but breeders produce dogs with a family likeness, so you can see which type you prefer. When judging has been completed, talk to the exhibitors and find out more about their dogs. They may not have puppies available, but some will be planning a litter, and you may decide to put your name on a waiting list.

Internet research

The Internet is an excellent resource, but when it comes to finding a puppy, use it with care:

DO go to the website of your national kennel club.

Both the American Kennel Club (AKC) and the Kennel Club (KC) have excellent websites which will give you information about the Weimaraner as a breed, and what to look for when choosing a puppy. You will also find contact details for specialist breed clubs (see below).

Both sites have lists of puppies available, and you can look out for breeders of merit (AKC) and assured breeders (KC) which indicates that a code of conduct has been adhered to.

DO find details of specialist breed clubs.

On breed club websites you will find lots of useful information which will help you to care for your Weimaraner.

There may be contact details of breeders in your area, or you may need to go through the club secretary. Some websites also have a list of breeders that have puppies available. The advantage of going through a breed club is that members will follow a code of ethics, and this will give you some guarantees regarding breeding stock and health checks.

If you are planning to show your Weimaraner you will obviously go to a breeder that has had some success in the ring, so you will need to do additional research to discover more about their breeding lines and the type of Weimaraner they produce.

Similarly, if you want to work your Weimaraner in the field, you should find a breeder who has specialised in producing this type of dog.

Unlike many of the other gundog breeds, such as

retrievers and spaniels, there is not a split between working dogs and show dogs in terms of physical appearance, but it makes sense to find bloodlines with proven working ability.

DO NOT look at puppies for sale.

There are legitimate Weimaraner breeders with their own websites, and they may, occasionally, advertise a litter, although in most cases reputable breeders have waiting lists for their puppies. The danger comes from unscrupulous breeders that produce puppies purely for profit, with no thought for the health of the dogs they breed from and no care given to rearing the litter.

Photos of puppies are hard to resist, but never make a decision based purely on an advertisement. You need to find out who the breeder is, and have the opportunity to visit their premises and inspect the litter before making a decision.

Questions, questions, questions

- When you find a breeder with puppies available, you will have lots of questions to ask. These should include the following:

- Where have the puppies been reared? Hopefully, they will be in a home environment which gives them the best possible start in life.

A caring breeder will be happy to answer all your questions.

- How many are in the litter?

- What is the split of males and females?

- How many have already been spoken for? The breeder will probably be keeping a puppy to show or for breeding, and there may be others on a waiting list.

- Can I see the mother with her puppies?

- What age are the puppies?

- When will they be ready to go to their new homes?

Bear in mind puppies need to be with their mother and siblings until they are eight weeks of age otherwise they miss out on vital learning and communication skills, which will have a detrimental effect on them for the rest of their lives. You should also be prepared to answer a number of searching questions so the breeder can check if you are suitable as a potential owner of one of their precious puppies. You will be asked some or all of the following questions:

- What is your home set up?

- Do you have children/grandchildren?

- What are their ages?

- Do you have a securely fenced garden?

- Is there somebody at home the majority of the time?

- What is your previous experience with dogs?

- Do you already have other dogs at home?

- Do you have plans to show or work your Weimaraner?

The breeder is not being intrusive; he needs to understand the type of home you will be able to provide in order to make the right match. Do not be offended by this; the breeder is doing it both for your, and the dog's, benefit. Steer clear of a breeder who does not ask you questions. He or she may be more interested in making money out of the puppies than ensuring that they go to good homes. They may also have taken other shortcuts which may prove disastrous, and very expensive, in terms of vet bills or plain heartache.

Health issues

In common with all pure-bred dogs, the Weimaraner suffers from some hereditary problems so you need to talk to the breeder about the health status of breeding stock and find out if there are any issues of concern. *See Breed specific conditions.*

Puppy watching

The piercing blue eyes of a Weimaraner puppy combined with his huge elephant ears are totally irresistible – you will probably find yourself wanting to take the whole litter home with you! However, you must not let your heart rule your head. Try to put your feelings to one side so that you can make an informed choice.

You need to be 100 per cent confident that the breeding stock is healthy, and the puppies have been reared with love and care, before making a commitment to buy.

Viewing a litter

It is a good idea to have a mental checklist of what to look out for when you visit a breeder. This is what you want to see:

- A clean, hygienic environment.

- Puppies who are out-going, friendly, and eager to meet you.

- A sweet-natured mother who is ready to show off her pups.

- Puppies that are well covered, but not pot-bellied, which could be an indication of worms.

- Bright eyes, with no sign of soreness or discharge.

- Clean ears that smell fresh.

- No discharge from the ears or the nose.

- Clean rear ends – matting could indicate an upset tummy.

It is important that you see the mother with her puppies as this will give you a good idea of the temperament they are likely to inherit. It is also helpful if you can see other close relatives so you can see the type of Weimaraner the breeder produces.

In most cases, you will not be able to see the father (sire) as most breeders will travel some distance to find a stud dog that is not too close to their own bloodlines and complements their bitch. However, you should be able to see photos of him and be given the chance to examine his pedigree and show record.

Companion puppy

If you are looking for a Weimaraner purely as a companion, you should be guided by the breeder who will have spent hours and hours puppy watching, and will know each of the pups as an individual. It is tempting to choose a puppy yourself, but the breeder will take into account your family set up and lifestyle and will help you pick the most suitable puppy.

Working/ sports puppy

If you are planning to work your Weimaraner in the field or compete in one of the canine sports, you will be looking for a puppy that is keen to play and to interact with people. This will be invaluable when you train him.

There are a few basic tests you can carry out which will help you assess working potential. These tests need to be carried out on each individual puppy:

- Get hold of a toy – or even a screwed up piece of paper – and throw it. A pup with a strong instinct to retrieve will run out and bring it back to you.

- Drop an object, such as a saucepan lid, when the puppy's attention is focused elsewhere. He should react to the noise but recover quickly. This will indicate that he is not too sound sensitive and will tolerate gunfire.

- Walk away from the pup and see if he follows. A working dog needs a degree of independence but he also needs to be people orientated.

Show puppy

If you are buying a puppy with the hope of showing him, make sure you make this clear to the breeder. A lot of planning goes into producing a litter, and although all the puppies will have been reared with equal care, there will be one or two that have show potential.

Ideally, recruit a breed expert to inspect the puppies with you so you have the benefit of their objective evaluation.

The breeder will also be there to help as they will want to ensure that only the best of their stock is exhibited in the show ring. Wait until the puppies are between seven and eight weeks before making your choice as this gives them time to develop.

It is impossible to say with certainty that a puppy is going to be successful in the show ring; puppies go through many stages when they are growing and the ugly duckling could well surprise you.

However, there are certain guidelines which are worth following:

- A puppy should appear to be balanced and show correct angulation in front and behind.

- The head should have the correct proportions – but do not be misled by the ears. They are huge in a puppy but by around five months of age you will get a better idea of the end result.

- Youngsters have blue eyes; the true colour does not come through until around 18 months of age.

- The tail set should be slightly below the back line to allow for the correct tail carriage.

It takes an expert eye to assess show potential.

A Weimaraner-friendly home

It may seem an age before your Weimaraner puppy is ready to leave the breeder and move to his new home. But you can fill the time by getting your home ready, and buying the equipment you will need. These preparations apply to a new puppy but, in reality, they are the means of creating an environment that is safe and secure for your Weimaraner throughout his life.

In the home

Nothing is safe when a puppy is about, and that is certainly true if you have a Weimaraner in the house! Everything is new and exciting for a young puppy, and he will investigate everything with his mouth, which can lead him into all sorts of mischief.

One thing is certain; a free-ranging Weimaraner puppy cannot be trusted. Remember, it is not only

your prized possessions that are under threat – the damage a puppy can inflict on himself is equally relevant. Trailing electric cables are a major hazard so these will need to be secured out of reach.

You will need to make sure all cupboards and storage units cannot be opened or broken into. This applies particularly in the kitchen where you may store cleaning materials, and other substances, which could be toxic to dogs. There are a number of household plants that are poisonous, so these will need to be relocated, along with breakable ornaments.

You may decide to declare upstairs off-limits and this is a sensible decision, particularly as negotiating stairs can be hazardous for a young puppy. The best way of doing this is to install a baby gate; these can also be useful if you want to limit your Weimaraner's freedom in any other part of the house. This barrier works well as your dog is separate but does not feel excluded from what is going on.

In the garden

The Weimaraner is a keen explorer and this could well include investigating what lies beyond your garden. For this reason, your garden will need to be securely fenced – a height of 1.5-1.8 metres (5-6 ft) is essential for a dog that is capable of jumping a five-bar gate. Some Weimaraners are great diggers, so fencing should be checked regularly in case your dog is trying to excavate his way out! If you have gates leading out of your property, they must have secure fastenings.

If you are a keen gardener, you may want to think about creating an area of garden that is free from plants and shrubs. A Weimaraner may share your passion for gardening but you are unlikely to appreciate his endeavours. Digging holes and uprooting plants is his idea of helping.

If you allow your Weimaraner free access to the garden you should be aware that there are a number of plants that are toxic to dogs, such as tulip bulbs, lily of the valley, azaleas, jasmine and daffodil flowers. You can find a comprehensive list on the Internet.

You also need to be aware that garden chemicals, such as fertilisers, fungicides and pesticides, are highly toxic so be very careful where you use them.

Swimming pools and ponds should be covered. A curious puppy will be drawn to investigate and may, unintentionally, find himself in the water. The danger is that although he may be able to swim, he will struggle to find his way out.

You will also need to designate a toileting area. This will assist the house training process, and it will also make cleaning up easier.

House rules

Before your puppy comes home, hold a family conference to make the house rules. You need to decide which rooms your puppy will have access to, and establish whether he is to be allowed on the furniture or not. It is important to start as you mean to go on. You cannot invite a puppy on to the sofa for cuddles only to decide in a few months' time that this is no longer desirable.

The Weimaraner likes to please, but he will push it if he doesn't know where his boundaries lie. If house rules are applied consistently, he will understand what is, and what is not, allowed, and he will learn to respect you and co-operate with you.

Buying equipment

There are some essential items of equipment you will need for your Weimaraner. If you choose wisely, much of it will last for many years to come.

Indoor crate

Rearing a puppy is so much easier if you invest in an

Facing page: Your Weimaraner needs to learn what is, and what is not, allowed.

indoor crate. It provides a safe haven for your puppy at night, when you have to go out during the day, and at other times when you cannot supervise him. A puppy needs a base where he feels safe and secure, and where he can rest undisturbed. An indoor crate provides the perfect den, and many adults continue to use them throughout their lives.

The crate needs to be big enough for an adult to be able to stand up, turn around, and stretch out in comfort. The correct sized crate for a female is 90 x 60 x 66cm (36 x 23.5 x 26in); a male needs more room so his crate should measure 105 x 71 x 76cm (41.5 x 28 x 30in).

You will also need to consider where you are going to locate the crate. The kitchen is usually the most suitable place as this is the hub of family life. Try to find a snug corner where the puppy can rest when he wants to, but where he can also see what is going on around him, and still be with the family.

Beds and bedding

The crate will need to be lined with bedding and the best type to buy is synthetic fleece. This is warm and cosy, and as moisture soaks through it, your puppy will not have a wet bed when he is tiny and is still unable to go through the night without relieving himself. This type of bedding is machine washable and easy to dry; buy two pieces, so you have one to use while the other piece is in the wash. If you have purchased a crate, you may not feel the need to buy an extra bed, although your Weimaraner may like to have a bed in the family room so he feels part of household activities.

There is an amazing array of dog-beds to chose from – duvets, bean bags, cushions, baskets, igloos, mini-four posters – so you can take your pick! However, you do need to bear in mind that a puppy may enjoy chewing his bed, so it is probably worth delaying this purchase until your Weimaraner has finished teething.

Collar and lead

You may think that it is not worth buying a collar for the first few weeks, but the sooner your pup gets used to it, the better. A nylon lightweight collar is recommended, as most puppies will accept it without making a fuss. Be careful when you are fitting the collar that is not too tight, but equally not too loose as slipping the collar can become a favourite game...

A matching webbing lead will be fine to begin with but as your Weimaraner grows you will need something more substantial. Again, there are plenty to choose from; the most important consideration is that the lead has a secure trigger fastening.

An extending lead can be a useful purchase as you can give your Weimaraner limited freedom when it is not safe or permitted to allow him off lead. However, you should never use it when walking alongside roads as an unexpected pull from your Weimaraner resulting in the lead extending further than you want, could have disastrous consequences.

ID

Your Weimaraner needs to wear some form of ID when he is out in public places. This can be in the form of a disc, engraved with your contact details, attached to the collar. When your Weimaraner is full-grown, you can buy an embroidered collar with your contact details, which eliminates the danger of the disc becoming detached from the collar.

Microchipping, which is a permanent form of ID, is now a legal requirement in the UK, and increasingly breeders are getting puppies micro chipped before they go to their new homes.

A microchip is the size of a grain of rice. It is injected under the skin, usually between the shoulder blades, with a special needle. It has tiny barbs on it, which dig into the tissue around where it lies, so it does not migrate from that spot.

Each chip has its own unique identification number

Facing page: You will need to consider a permanent form of ID.

which can only be read by a special scanner. That ID number is then registered on a national database with your name and details, so that if ever your dog is lost, he can be taken to any vet or rescue centre where he is scanned and then you are contacted.

If your puppy has not been micro chipped, you can ask your vet to do it, maybe when he goes for his vaccinations.

Bowls

Your Weimaraner will need two bowls; one for food, and one for fresh drinking water, which should always be readily available.

A stainless steel bowl is a good choice for food as it is tough and hygienic. Plastic bowls will almost certainly be chewed, and there is a danger that bacteria can collect in the small cracks that may appear.

You can opt for a second stainless steel bowl for drinking water, or you may prefer a heavier ceramic bowl which will not be knocked over so easily.

Food

The breeder will let you know what your puppy is eating and should provide a full diet sheet to guide you through the first six months of your puppy's feeding regime – how much they are eating per meal, how many meals per day, when to increase the amounts given per meal and when to reduce the meals per day.

The breeder may provide you with some food when you go and collect your puppy, but it is worth making enquiries in advance about the availability of the brand that is recommended.

Grooming gear

The Weimaraner is a fairly low maintenance breed in terms of coat but there are a few essentials you will need:

- Soft brush to use while your puppy is becoming accustomed to grooming.

For short-haired

- Hound glove/rubber curry comb for adult coat care.

For long-haired

- Soft bristle brush

- Fine-toothed metal comb

- Nail-clippers – the guillotine type are easy to use.

- Toothbrush and toothpaste: Choose between a long-handled toothbrush or a finger brush

The Weimaraner is an adaptable breed and will soon fit into your family and your lifestyle.

– whichever you find easiest to use. There are flavoured canine toothpastes on the market which are acceptable to your dog.

Toys

Weimaraner puppies love to play, and there is no shortage of dog toys on the market.

But before you get carried away with buying a vast range of toys to keep your puppy entertained, think about possible hazards.

A puppy can easily chew bits from soft or plastic toys, and if this material is ingested it can cause serious problems in the form of a blockage.

This is particularly true of toys with squeakers; a Weimaraner will show amazing determination and will keep on chewing (and squeaking the toy) until he eventually removes the squeaker.

The safest toys to choose are made of hard rubber; a rubber kong which can be stuffed with food is ideal.

You can also buy rope tug toys, but be careful how you play with your dog, particularly while he is teething, which occurs at around four months.

Finding a vet

Before your puppy arrives home, you should register with a vet. Visit several vets in your local area, or speak to other pet owners that you might know, to see who they recommend.

It is so important to find a good vet – almost as much as finding a good doctor for yourself.

You need to find someone with whom you can build up a good rapport and have complete faith in. Word of mouth is really the best recommendation.

When you contact a veterinary practice, find out the following:

- Does the surgery run an appointment system?
- What are the arrangements for emergency, out of hours cover?
- Do any of the vets in the practice have experience treating Weimaraners?
- What facilities are available at the practice?

If you are satisfied with what you find, and the staff appear to be helpful and friendly, book an appointment so your puppy can have a health check a couple of days after you collect him.

Settling in

When you first arrive home with your puppy, be careful not to overwhelm him. You and your family are hugely excited, but the puppy is in a completely strange environment with new sounds, smells and sights, which is a daunting experience, even for the boldest of pups.

Some puppies are very confident, wanting to play straightaway and quickly making friends; others need a little longer. Keep a close check on your puppy's body language and reactions so you can proceed at a pace he is comfortable with.

First, let him explore the garden. He will probably need to relieve himself after the journey home, so take him to the allocated toileting area and, when he performs, give him plenty of praise. When you take your puppy indoors, let him investigate again. Show him his crate, and encourage him to go in by throwing in a treat. Let him have a sniff, and allow him to go in and out as he wants to. Later on, when

he is tired, you can put him in the crate while you stay in the room. In this way he will learn to settle and will not think he is being abandoned.

It is a good idea to feed your puppy in his crate, at least to begin with, as this helps to build up a positive association.

It will not be long before your Weimaraner sees his crate as his own special den and will go there as a matter of choice. Some owners place a blanket over the crate, covering the back and sides, so that it is even more cosy and den-like.

Meeting the family

Resist the temptation of inviting friends and neighbours to come and meet the new arrival; your puppy needs to focus on getting to know his new family for the first few days. Try not to swamp your Weimaraner with too much attention; give him a chance to explore and find his feet. There will be plenty of time for cuddles later on!

If you have children in the family, you need to keep everything as calm as possible. Your puppy may not have met children before, and even if he has, he will still find them strange and unpredictable.

A puppy can become alarmed by too much noise, or he may go to the opposite extreme and become over-excited, which can lead to mouthing and nipping. The best plan is to get the children to sit on the floor and give them all a treat. Each child can then call the puppy, stroke him, and offer a treat. In this way the puppy is making the decisions rather than being forced into interactions he may find stressful. If he tries to nip or mouth, make sure there is a toy at the ready, so his attention can be diverted to something he is allowed to bite. If you do this consistently, he will learn to inhibit his desire to mouth when he is interacting with people.

Right from the start, impose a rule that the children are not allowed to pick up or carry the puppy. They can cuddle him when they are sitting on the floor. This may sound a little severe, but a wriggly puppy can be dropped in an instant, sometimes with disastrous consequences.

If possible, try to make sure your Weimaraner is only given attention when he has all four feet on the ground. That sweet little puppy will soon become a powerful adult and you need to establish the fact that jumping up is non-productive. Involve all family members with the day-to-day care of your puppy; this will enable the bond to develop with the whole family as opposed to just one person. Encourage the children to train and reward the puppy, teaching him to follow their commands without question.

The animal family

Care must be taken when introducing a puppy to a resident dog to ensure that relations get off on the right footing. Weimaraners are sociable dogs and you will rarely have problems, but it is better to be safe rather than sorry.

Your adult dog may be allowed to meet the puppy at the breeder's, which is ideal as the older dog will not feel threatened if he is away from home. But if this is not possible, allow your dog to smell the puppy's bedding (the bedding supplied by the breeder is fine) before they actually meet so he familiarises himself with the puppy's scent.

The garden is the best place for introducing the puppy, as the adult will regard it as neutral territory. He will probably take a great interest in the puppy and sniff him all over.

Most puppies are naturally submissive in this situation, and your pup may lick the other dog's mouth or roll over on to his back. Try not to interfere as this is the way that dogs get to know each other.

You will only need to intervene if the older dog is too boisterous, and alarms the puppy. In this case, it is a good idea to put the adult on his lead so you have some measure of control.

It rarely takes long for an adult to accept a puppy, as he does not constitute a threat. This will be underlined if you make a big fuss of the older dog so that he has no reason to feel jealous. But no matter how well the two dogs are getting on, do not leave them alone unless one is crated.

Feline friends

The Weimaraner is a hunting dog, and this should not be forgotten if you have a cat in the family. If a cat runs, a Weimaraner will chase. If you prevent this scenario from the onset, your Weimaraner will learn to tolerate the cat and they will live in harmony.

It may be easier if the cat is confined in a carrier for the first couple of meetings so your puppy has a chance to make his acquaintance in a controlled situation.

The Weimaraner is a friendly, out-going dog who will enjoy canine company.

Keep calling your puppy to you and rewarding him so that he does not focus too intently on the cat.

You can then graduate to holding your puppy while the cat is free, again rewarding him with a treat every time he responds to you and looks away from the cat. When you allow your puppy to go free, make sure the cat has an easy escape route, just in case he tries to chase.

This is an on-going process, but all the time your Weimaraner is learning that he is rewarded for ignoring the cat. In time, the novelty will wear off and the pair will mostly ignore each other.

In some cases, a Weimaraner and the family cat will become the best of friends and end up sharing a bed!

If you supervise initial interactions between the two species, you will establish the basis for a sound, stress-free relationship.

Feeding

The breeder will generally provide enough food for the first few days so the puppy does not have to cope with a change in diet – and possible digestive upset – along with all the stress of moving home.

Some puppies eat up their food from the first meal onwards, others are more concerned by their new surroundings and are too distracted to eat. Most Weimaraners are pretty keen on their food so it is rare to have on-going problems.

However if your puppy seems disinterested in his food, give him 10 minutes to eat what he wants and then remove the leftovers and start afresh at the next meal. Obviously if you have any concerns about your puppy in the first few days, seek advice from your vet.

It is important to give your dog space where he can eat in peace, and if you have children, you need to establish a rule that no one is to go near the dog when he is feeding.

However, the Weimaraner does have a guarding streak so you must ensure that he does not become possessive about his food.

The best strategy is to give him half his ration, and then drop food around his bowl. This will stop him guarding his bowl and, at the same time, he will see your presence in a positive light.

You can also call him away from the bowl and reward him with food – maybe something extra special – which he can take from your hand. Start doing this as soon as your puppy arrives in his new home, and continue working on it throughout his life.

The first night

Your puppy will have spent the first weeks of his life with either his mother or curled up with his siblings. He is then taken from everything he knows as familiar, lavished with attention by his new family, and then comes bed time when he is left all alone. It is little wonder that he feels abandoned.

The best plan is to establish a nighttime routine, and then stick to it so that your puppy knows what is expected of him. Take your puppy out into the garden to relieve himself, and then settle him in his crate.

Some people leave a low light on for the puppy at night for the first week, others have tried a radio as company or a ticking clock.

A covered hot-water bottle, filled with warm water, can also be a comfort. Like people, puppies are all individuals and what works for one, does not necessarily work for another, so it is a matter of trial and error.

Be very positive when you leave your puppy on his own; do not linger, or keep returning; this will make the situation more difficult.

It is inevitable that he will protest to begin with, but if you stick to your routine, he will accept that he gets left at night but you always return in the morning.

Rescued dogs

Settling an older, rescued dog in the home is very similar to a puppy in as much as you will need to make the same preparations regarding his homecoming.

As with a puppy, an older dog will need you to be consistent, so start as you mean to go on.

There is often an initial honeymoon period when you bring a rescued dog home, where he will be on his best behaviour for the first few weeks.

It is after these first couple of weeks that the true nature of the dog will show, so be prepared for subtle changes in his behaviour.

It may be advisable to register with a reputable training club, so you can seek advice on any training or behavioural issues at an early stage.

Above all, remember that a rescued dog ceases to be a rescued dog the moment he enters his forever home and should be treated normally like any other family pet.

Facing page: A rescued dog needs special care and understanding.

House training

This is an aspect of training that first-time owners dread, but if you start as you mean to go on, it will not be long before your Weimaraner understands what is required.

The key to successful house training is vigilance and consistency. If you establish a routine, and you stick to it, your puppy will soon get the hang of it.

Equally, you must be there to supervise him at all times, except when he is safely tucked up in his crate. It is when a puppy is left to wander from room to room that accidents are most likely to happen.

As discussed earlier, you will have allocated a toileting area in your garden when preparing for your puppy's homecoming.

You need to take your puppy to this area every time

he needs to relieve himself so he builds up an association and knows why you have brought him out to the garden.

Establish a routine and make sure you take your puppy out at the following times:

- First thing in the morning

- After mealtimes

- On waking from a sleep

- Following a play session

- Last thing at night.

A puppy should be taken out to relieve himself every two hours as an absolute minimum. If you can manage an hourly trip out, so much the better.

The more often your puppy gets it right, the quicker he will learn to be clean in the house. It helps if you use a verbal cue, such as 'Busy', when your pup is performing and, in time, this will trigger the desired response.

Do not be tempted to put your puppy out on the doorstep in the hope that he will toilet on his own. Most pups simply sit there, waiting to get back inside the house!

No matter how bad the weather is, accompany your puppy and give him lots of praise when he performs correctly.

Do not rush back inside as soon as he has finished; your puppy might start to delay in the hope of prolonging his time outside with you. Praise him, have a quick game, and then you can both return indoors.

When accidents happen

No matter how vigilant you are, there are bound to be accidents. If you witness the accident, take your puppy outside immediately, and give him lots of praise if he finishes his business out there.

If you are not there when he has an accident, do not scold him when you discover what has happened. He will not remember what he has done and will not understand why you are cross with him. Simply clean it up and resolve to be more vigilant next time.

Make sure you use a deodoriser, available in pet stores, when you clean up otherwise your pup will be drawn to the smell and may be tempted to use the same spot again.

Choosing a diet

There are so many different types of dog food on sale, all claiming to be the best, so how do you know what is likely to suit your Weimaraner?

When choosing a diet, there are basically three categories to choose from:

Complete

This is probably the most popular diet as it is easy to feed and is specially formulated with all the nutrients your dog needs. This means that you should not add any supplements or you may upset the nutritional balance.

Most complete diets come in different life stages: puppy, adult maintenance and senior, so this means that your Weimaraner is getting what he needs when he is growing, during adulthood, and as he becomes older. You can even get prescription diets for dogs

with particular health issues.

Check protein levels provided in the diet; it is important that your Weimaraner has the correct level depending on his age and lifestyle.

Puppies and juniors needs 25-35 per cent of protein in the diet for growth and development; 18-20 per cent protein is adequate for adult maintenance; working dogs and lactating bitches need a higher level, around 28-25 per cent, and veterans needs a much lower level, decreasing from the basic adult maintenance diet.

There are many different brands to choose from so it is advisable to seek advice from your puppy's breeder who will have lengthy experience of feeding Weimaraners.

Canned/pouches

This type of food is usually fed with hard biscuit, and most Weimaraners find it very appetising. However, the ingredients and the nutritional value do vary significantly between the different brands so you will need to check the label. This type of food often has a high moisture content, so you need to be sure your Weimaraner is getting all the nutrition he needs.

Homemade

There are some owners who like to prepare meals especially for their dogs – and it is probably much appreciated. The danger is that although the food is tasty, and your Weimaraner may appreciate the variety, you cannot be sure that it has the correct nutritional balance.

If this is a route you want to go down, you will need to find out the exact ratio of fats, carbohydrates, proteins, minerals and vitamins that are needed, which is quite an undertaking.

The Barf (Biologically Appropriate Raw Food) diet is another, more natural approach to feeding. Dogs are fed a diet mimicking what they would have eaten in the wild, consisting of raw meat, bone, muscle, fat, and vegetable matter. Weimaraners do well on this diet so it is certainly worthy of consideration. There are now a number of companies that specialise in producing the Barf diet in frozen form, which will make your job a lot easier.

Feeding regime

When your puppy arrives in his new home he will need four meals, evenly spaced throughout the day. You may decide to keep to the diet recommended by your puppy's breeder, and if your pup is thriving there is no need to change. However, if your puppy is not doing well on the food, or you have problems with supply, you will need to make a change.

When switching diets, it is very important to do it on a gradual basis, changing over from one food to the next, a little at a time, and spreading the transition over a week to 10 days. This will avoid the risk of digestive upset.

From about 12 weeks, you can go down to three meals a day, and by six months, you can feed twice daily – a regime which should suit your Weimaraner for the rest of his life. There are those that advocate feeding one meal a day, but this may increase the likelihood of gastric torsion, also known as bloat.

This is a life threatening condition where the gut twists and fills with air. Emergency surgery is the only hope of survival. It is thought that overloading the stomach could be a potential risk, and exercising immediately before and after feeding should be avoided. To err on the side of caution, leave a minimum of one hour either side of exercise.

Faddy feeders

In common with most of the gundog breeds, the Weimaraner is not fussy about his food. He has a good appetite; if this changes it could be a sign that he is unwell and you may need to seek advice. However, there will always be the Weimaraner who thinks it is worth pushing his luck in the hope that you may provide superior food.

The active Weimaraner needs a well-balanced, high-quality diet.

One look from those haunting eyes is enough to melt your heart, stirring you to greater efforts to find a food that your Weimaraner will really like. At first you may add some gravy, then you may try some chicken... A clever Weimaraner will quickly realise that if he holds out, tastier treats will follow.

This is a bad game to play as not only will you run out of tempting delicacies, you will also be losing your Weimaraner's respect.

If your Weimaraner is turning up his nose at mealtimes, give him 10 minutes to eat what he wants, and then take up his bowl. Do not feed him treats in between meals, and give him fresh food at his next mealtime.

If you continue this regime for a couple of days, your Weimaraner will realise that there is no percentage in holding out for better food as it never materialises. In most cases, this is just a 'trying it on' phase, and if you cope with common sense, you will soon return to the status quo and your Weimaraner will be content with his normal rations. If, however, your dog refuses all food for more than 24 hours you need to observe his behaviour to see if there are any signs of ill health, which may involve the need for a veterinary check up.

Bones and chews

Puppies love to chew, and many adults also enjoy gnawing on a bone. A raw marrow bone is ideal, but make sure it is always given under supervision.

White, sterilised bones do not make so much mess as a raw marrow bone, and they have the same end result of helping to keep your dog's teeth clean. Rawhide chews are best avoided; it is all too easy for a Weimaraner to bite off a chunk and swallow it, with the danger of it then causing a blockage.

Ideal weight

In order to help to keep your Weimaraner in good health it is necessary to monitor his weight. If your dog gets sufficient exercise and is fed a diet that matches his energy output, he should not put on weight.

But it is something you should watch closely. A dog that is carrying too much weight is vulnerable to many health issues; he has a reduced quality of life as he cannot exercise properly, and he will almost certainly have a reduced life expectancy.

When judging your Weimaraner's condition, look at him from above, and make sure you can see a definite waist. You should be able to feel his ribs, but not see them.

If you are concerned about your Weimaraner's weight, get into the habit of visiting your veterinary surgery on a monthly basis so that you can weigh him. You can keep a record of his weight so you can make adjustments if necessary.

If you are worried that your Weimaraner is putting on too much weight, or equally if you think he is underweight, consult your vet who will help you to plan a suitable diet.

Caring for your Weimaraner

The Weimaraner is classed as a low maintenance breed but, like all animals, he has his own special needs which you must take on board.

Coat care

The Weimaraner may be long-haired or short-haired which impacts on the amount of grooming that is required.

Short-haired

A short-haired Weimaraner needs minimal grooming – and a puppy requires even less – but do not make the mistake of ignoring this aspect of his care.

A grooming session gives you the opportunity to check your dog and to discover any minor problems, such as sore places, or any abnormalities, such as lumps and bumps, which may need to be investigated.

Remember, if you spot a problem early on, you increase the chance of an early diagnosis and successful treatment.

The first step is to get your puppy used to being handled so that he accepts the attention without resentment. Initially, he will wriggle and attempt to mouth you, but just ignore his protests.

Hold him steady for a few moments, and reward him when he is still. A puppy needs to learn that it is OK to be touched all over; if you fail to do this, he may try to warn you off by growling, which could develop into more problematic behaviour.

Start by handling your puppy all over, stroking him from his head to his tail. Lift up each paw in turn, and reward him with a treat when he co-operates.

Then roll him over on to his back and tickle his tummy; this is a very vulnerable position for a dog to adopt, so do not force the issue.

Be firm but gentle, and give your Weimaraner lots of praise when he does as you ask.

When your Weimaraner is happy to be handled in this way, you can introduce a soft brush and spend a few minutes working on his coat, and then reward him.

He will gradually learn to accept the attention, and will relax while you groom him.

When the adult coat comes through it will be short, smooth and dense; there is no undercoat. A rubber curry comb or body brush is ideal for keeping the coat in good order.

It gets rid of dirt and debris and brushing also has a massaging effect.

A rubber curry comb is also useful for getting rid of dead hair when your Weimaraner is shedding his coat.

If you are exhibiting your Weimaraner in the show

ring, or you want him to look his very best, give him a rub down with a chamois leather – this will really bring out the sheen in his coat.

Long-haired

There is more work involved in grooming a long-haired Weimaraner, and grooming sessions need to be more frequent.

Brushing and combing the coat two or three times a week will keep your Weimaraner's coat looking good and tangle free.

A soft bristle brush works best on this type of coat. After you have finished brushing, go over the coat again using a fine-toothed metal comb.

Pay particular attention to the feathering on the ears, the neck, the chest and belly, the back of the legs and the tail.

Bathing

A Weimaraner should not be bathed too frequently as it has an adverse effect on the skin's natural oils. Not only does this result in a dull coat, it can also cause dry, itchy skin.

However, there are times when your Weimaraner decides to roll in something particularly revolting, and you have no option but to bath him.

Make sure you use a mild moisturising shampoo
specially formulated for dogs, and you can also
use a conditioner which will improve the quality
and appearance of the coat. It is a good idea to
plan your first bath while your Weimaraner is still
small enough to handle easily. He will then become
accustomed to the procedure and bath times will not
become a battlefield.

*Grooming gives you
the opportunity to keep
a close check on your
Weimaraner.*

Routine care

In addition to grooming, you will need to carry out some routine care.

Eyes

Check the eyes for signs of soreness or discharge. You can use a piece of cotton wool (cotton) – a separate piece for each eye – and wipe away any debris.

Ears

The ears should be clean and free from odour. You can buy specially manufactured ear wipes, or you can use a piece of cotton wool to clean them if necessary. Do not probe into the ear canal or you risk doing more harm than good.

Teeth

Dental disease is becoming more prevalent among dogs so teeth cleaning should be seen as an essential part of your care regime. The build up of tartar on the teeth can result in tooth decay, gum infection and bad breath, and if it is allowed to accumulate, you may have no option but to get the teeth cleaned under anaesthetic.

When your Weimaraner is still a puppy, accustom

Ears should be inspected and cleaned when necessary.

Regular brushing keeps teeth clean and gums healthy.

Accustom your Weimaraner to nail-clipping from an early age.

him to teeth cleaning so it becomes a matter of routine. Dog toothpaste comes in a variety of meaty flavours, which your Weimaraner will like, so you can start by putting some toothpaste on your finger and gently rubbing his teeth. You can then progress to using a finger brush or a toothbrush, whichever you find most convenient.

Remember to reward your Weimaraner when he co-operates and then he will positively look forward to his teeth-cleaning sessions.

Nails

Nail trimming is a task dreaded by many owners, and many dogs, but if you start early on, your Weimaraner will get used to the task you have to perform and will not fight against it. If you look closely you will be able to see the quick (the vein that runs through the nail), which you must avoid at all costs. If you cut the quick it will bleed profusely and cause considerable discomfort.

The best policy is to trim little and often so the nails don't grow too long, and you do not risk cutting too much and catching the quick.If you are worried about trimming your Weimaraner's nails, go to your vet so you can see it done properly. If you are still concerned, you can always use the services of a professional groomer.

Exercise

The Weimaraner was bred to hunt all day, moving with speed and using his natural agility to clear walls and work through the undergrowth. To do this he needs a huge amount of stamina, a trait which remains very much part of his physical make up.

An adult Weimaraner needs extensive exercise but do not get too carried away while your Weimaraner is growing. This is a time when bones and joints are vulnerable to injury so too much exercise, or undue stress and strain, such as climbing stairs or jumping in and out of the back of a car, should be avoided.

Initially your Weimaraner puppy will get as much exercise as he needs playing in the garden.

Once his inoculation programme has been completed he can go out on short lead-walking excursions for socialising purposes with 10 minutes' free running. This can be stepped up gradually, month by month, until he is physically mature.

Two 30-minute walks a day should be considered a minimum for an adult Weimaraner. This can be a mixture of lead walking and free running.

The Weimaraner has an outstanding sense of smell so he will relish the opportunity of going to new places and investigating new surroundings.

The working Weimaraner was expected to retrieve from water, and he is a strong and enthusiastic swimmer. If you have access to water he will enjoy playing retrieve – and you will certainly tire of it first!

Before allowing your Weimaraner to swim, make sure the water is safe with no strong currents, and check that there is an easy exit from the water.

Physical exercise is important, but you also need to exercise your Weimaraner's brain. Playing games such as retrieve and hide-and-seek is an excellent way of doing this.

The older Weimaraner

We are fortunate that the Weimaraner has a pretty good life expectancy – generally around 12 years, and some may do slightly better.

As your Weimaraner grows older, he may sleep more and he may be reluctant to go for longer walks. He may show signs of stiffness when he gets up from his bed, but these generally ease when he starts moving.

Some older Weimaraners may have impaired vision, and some may become a little deaf, but as long as their senses do not deteriorate dramatically, this is something older dogs learn to live with.

Facing page: Plan an exercise regime that suits your Weimaraner's age and lifestyle.

If you treat your older dog with kindness and consideration, he will enjoy his later years and suffer the minimum of discomfort.

It is advisable to switch him over to a senior diet, which is more suited to his needs, and you may need to adjust the quantity, as he will not be burning up the calories as he did when he was younger and more energetic.

The older Weimaraner will often prefer a softer diet, and you will need to keep a close check on his teeth as these may cause problems.

Make sure his sleeping quarters are warm and free from draughts, and if he gets wet, make sure you dry him thoroughly. Most important of all, be guided by your Weimaraner. He will have good days when he feels up to going for a walk, and other days when he would prefer to potter in the garden.

If you have a younger dog at home, this may well stimulate your Weimaraner to take more of an interest in what is going on, but do make sure that he is not pestered as he needs to rest undisturbed when he is tired.

Letting go

Inevitably there comes a time when your Weimaraner is not enjoying a good quality of life, and you need to make the painful decision to let him go.

We would all wish that our dogs died, painlessly, in their sleep but, unfortunately, this is rarely the case.

However, we can allow our dogs to die with dignity, and to suffer as a little as possible, and this should be our way of saying thank you for the wonderful companionship they have given us.

When you feel the time is drawing close, talk to your vet who will be able to make an objective assessment of your Weimaraner's condition and will help you to make the right decision.

This is the hardest thing you will ever have to do as a dog owner, and it is only natural to grieve for your beloved Weimaraner.

But eventually you will be able to look back on the happy memories of times spent together, and this will bring much comfort. You may, in time, feel that your life is not complete without a Weimaraner, and you will feel ready to welcome a new puppy into your home.

Social skills

To live in the modern world, without fears and anxieties, your Weimaraner needs to receive an education in social skills so that he learns to cope calmly and confidently in a wide variety of situations. The Weimaraner is an outgoing dog, with few hang-ups, and will relish the opportunity to broaden his horizons.

Early learning

The breeder will have begun a programme of socialisation by getting the puppies used to all the sights and sounds of a busy household.

You need to continue this when your pup arrives in his new home, making sure he is not worried by household equipment, such as the vacuum cleaner or the washing machine, and that he gets used to unexpected noises from the radio and television.

To begin with, your puppy needs to get used to all the members of his new family, but then you should give him the opportunity to meet friends and other people who visit your home.

If you do not have children, make sure your puppy has the chance to meet and play with other people's children, ensuring interactions are always supervised, so he learns that people come in small sizes too.

The Weimaraner is a friendly dog and enjoys the comings and goings of a busy household. However, there are two considerations to bear in mind.

A young, exuberant Weimaraner can be pushy when it comes to getting attention and he may decide that jumping up is part of his meeting and greeting strategy. You also need to bear in mind that the

Weimaraner has a protective streak and this may become apparent when visitors come to the house. It is your job to teach your Weimaraner good manners so that he remains calm and does not feel that visitors pose a threat.

Adopt the following training programme:

If your Weimaraner jumps up at you, demanding attention, simply ignore him. Turn away and do not speak to him – even to tell him off – as he will regard this as another form of attention.

Wait until he is calm and quiet, with all four feet on the ground, and then reward him by giving him attention and maybe asking him to "sit" for a treat.

You will need to be completely consistent in your training and repeat this lesson continually so that your Weimaraner learns that his attention-seeking strategies do not work. He will only get attention when you are ready to give it.

If visitors come to the house, keep your Weimaraner on a lead and make sure he is sitting before the visitor gives him attention. As your Weimaraner learns to control his behaviour you can ask the visitor to give him a treat when he has all four feet on the ground.

If your Weimaraner is showing guarding behaviour

when visitors come to the house, adopt the same strategy outlined above, firstly rewarding your Weimaraner for being calm and quiet and then allowing the visitor to give him a treat.

In this way, you are making the decisions and your Weimaraner will accept your leadership rather than taking the law into his own hands.

The outside world

When your puppy has completed his vaccinations, he is ready to venture into the outside world. Weimaraners are generally pretty confident but there is a lot for a youngster to take on board, so do not swamp him with too many new experiences when you first set out.

Obviously you need to work at lead-training before you go on your first expedition. There will be plenty of distractions to cope with, so you do not want additional problems of coping with a dog that is pulling or lagging on the lead.

Hopefully, you can set off with your Weimaraner walking by your side on a loose lead.

He may need additional encouragement when you venture further afield, so arm yourself with some extra special treats, which will give him a good reason to focus on you when required!

Start socialising your puppy in a quiet area with light traffic, and only progress to a busier place when he is ready. There is so much to see and hear – people (maybe carrying bags or umbrellas), pushchairs, bicycles, cars, lorries, machinery – so give your puppy a chance to take it all in.

A well-socialised Weimaraner will take all new situations in his stride.

If he does appear worried, do not fall into the trap of sympathising with him or over-doing the reassurance.

This will only teach your pup that he had a good reason to be worried and, with luck, you will rescue him if he feels scared.

Instead, give him a little space so he does not have to confront whatever he is frightened of, and distract him with a few treats.

Then encourage him to walk past, using an encouraging tone of voice, never forcing him by yanking on the lead.

Reward him for any forward movement, and your puppy will soon learn that he can trust you, and there is nothing to fear.

Your pup also needs to continue his education in canine manners, started by his mother and by his littermates, as he needs to be able to greet all dogs calmly, giving the signals that say he is friendly and offers no threat.

If you have a friend who has a dog of sound temperament, this is an ideal way to get your puppy used to social interactions. As your Weimaraner gets older and more established, you can widen his circle of canine acquaintances.

Training classes

A training class will give your Weimaraner the
opportunity to work alongside other dogs in a
controlled situation, and he will also learn to focus
on you in a different, distracting environment. Both
these lessons will be vital as your dog matures.
However, the training class needs to be of the
highest calibre or you risk doing more harm than
good. Before you go along with your puppy, attend
a class as an observer to make sure you are happy
with what goes on.

Find out the following:

- How much training experience do the instructors
  have?

- Are the classes divided into appropriate age
  categories?

- Do the instructors have experience training
  Weimaraners?

- Do they use positive, reward-based training
  methods?

If the training class is well run, it is certainly worth
attending. Both you and your Weimaraner will learn
useful training exercises; it will increase his social
skills, and you will have the chance to talk to lots of
like-minded dog enthusiasts.

Training guidelines

The Weimaraner is a highly intelligent dog and he relishes the opportunity to use his brain and to interact with members of his human family. Training, even at a basic level, is essential as a Weimaraner will become bored and hard to manage if he is deprived of mental stimulation and is uncertain of his status in the family pack.

You will be keen to get started but in your rush to get training underway, do not neglect the fundamentals which could make the difference between success and failure.

You need to get into the mindset of a Weimaraner, working out what motivates him and, equally, what makes him switch off.

Decide on your priorities for training, and then think

of ways of making your training as much fun – and as positive – as possible.

When you start training, try to observe the following guidelines:

Choose an area that is free from distractions so your puppy will focus on you. You can move on to a more challenging environment as your pup progresses.

Do not train your puppy just after he has eaten or when you have returned from exercise. He will either be too full, or too tired, to concentrate.

Do not train if you are in a bad mood, or if you are short of time. These sessions always end in disaster!

Providing a worthwhile reward is an essential tool in training. The Weimaraner will work for a toy and for treats so you can employ a flexible approach depending on what you are teaching.

If you decide to use a toy, make sure it is only brought out for training sessions so that it accrues added value.

Keep your verbal cues simple, and make sure you are consistent with the cues you use. For example, when you ask your puppy to go into the down position, the cue is "down", not "lie down, "get down", or anything else.

Remember, your Weimaraner does not speak English; he associates the sound of the word with the action.

If your dog is finding an exercise difficult, break it down into small steps so it is easier to understand. A Weimaraner can dig in his heels so you need to think creatively and give frequent rewards.

Do not make your training sessions boring and repetitious; your Weimaraner will lose concentration and will cease to co-operate.

Do not train for too long, particularly with a young puppy, who has a very short attention span, and always end training sessions on a positive note.

This does not necessarily mean getting an exercise right. If your pup is tired and making mistakes, ask him to do a simple exercise so you have the opportunity to praise and reward him.

You may well find that he benefits from having a break and will make better progress next time you try.

Above all, make training fun so you and your Weimaraner enjoy spending quality time together.

First lessons

Like all puppies, a young Weimaraner will soak up new experiences like a sponge, so training should start from the time your pup arrives in his new home.

Wearing a collar

You may, or may not, want your Weimaraner to wear a collar all the time. But when he goes out in public places he will need to be on a lead, and so he should be used to the feel of a collar around his neck. The best plan is to accustom your pup to wearing a soft collar for a few minutes at a time until he gets used to it.

Fit the collar so that you can get at least two fingers between the collar and his neck. Then have a game to distract his attention. This will work for a few moments; then he will stop, put his back leg up behind his neck and scratch away at the peculiar itchy thing which feels so odd.

Bend down, rotate the collar, pat him on the head

and distract him by playing with a toy or giving him a treat. Once he has worn the collar for a few minutes each day, he will soon ignore it and become used to it.

Remember, never leave the collar on the puppy unsupervised, especially when he is outside in the garden, or when he is in his crate, as it is could get snagged, causing serious injury.

Walking on the lead

This is a simple exercise but the Weimaraner is a powerful dog who likes to live life in the fast lane. It is therefore a good idea to master the basics, and for your Weimaraner to learn good lead walking manners before problems with pulling arise.

Once your puppy is used to the collar, take him outside into your secure garden where there are no distractions.

Attach the lead and, to begin with, allow him to wander with the lead trailing, making sure it does not become snagged. Then pick up the lead and follow the pup where he wants to go; he needs to get used to the sensation of being attached to you.

The next stage is to get your Weimaraner to follow you, and for this you will need some treats. To give yourself the best chance of success, make sure the treats are high value – cheese, sausage or cooked liver – so your Weimaraner is motivated to work with you. Show him you have a treat in your hand, and then encourage him to follow you.

Walk a few paces, and if he is walking with you, stop and reward him. If he puts on the brakes, simply change direction and lure him with the treat.

Next, introduce some changes of direction so your puppy is walking confidently alongside you. At this stage, introduce a verbal cue – "heel" – when your puppy is in the correct position. You can then graduate to walking your puppy outside the home, as long as he has completed his vaccination programme, starting in quiet areas and building up to busier environments.

Training strategy

Some young Weimaraners decide that pulling on the lead is a good option, and, in no time, the dog is taking you for a walk. This soon becomes an unpleasant experience, so it is important to adopt a strategy that makes your Weimaraner realise there is absolutely no percentage in pulling.

Restrict lead training to the garden in the initial stages so you are working in an environment that is free from distractions.

Walk a few paces, being very aware of any tension on the lead. If you feel the lead tighten and your Weimaraner is attempting to get ahead of you, stop, change direction, and set off again.

Your Weimaraner needs to understand that pulling ahead has exactly the opposite effect to the one he wants. Rather than calling the tune, he has to co-operate with you.

Keep a good supply of tasty treats and remember only reward – with food and with verbal praise - when he is walking on a loose lead by your side.

The mistake made by many owners at this stage is to use the treats to lure the dog into position rather than rewarding him for the correct behaviour.

Keep training sessions short, and when you are ready to venture into the outside world, do not be too ambitious to begin with. Build up the level of distraction and the duration of lead walking only when your Weimaraner is consistently showing the behaviour you want.

Facing page: A well trained Weimaraner is a pleasure to own.

Come when called

The Weimaraner is fundamentally an obedient dog who enjoys being with his family. However there are times when he gets distracted. There are so many enticing smells, places to explore, people and dogs to meet... He will never stray too far away, but he may get into the habit of coming in his own time unless you make the recall a rewarding exercise.

Your aim must be to make coming when called even more rewarding than whatever is on your Weimaraner's personal agenda.

This needs to be built up over a period of time, with lots of repetition, so your Weimaraner sees you as a fun person that is always ready to reward him, rather than as an irate owner who is trying to spoil his fun.

Hopefully, the breeder will have laid the foundations simply by calling the puppies to "come" when it is dinnertime, or when they are moving from one place to another.

You can build on this when your puppy arrives in his new home, calling him to "come" when he is in a confined space, such as the kitchen. This is a good place to build up a positive association with the verbal cue – particularly if you ask your puppy to "come" to get his dinner!

The next stage is to transfer the lesson to the garden. Arm yourself with some treats, and wait until your puppy is distracted.

Then call him, using a higher-pitched, excited tone of voice. At this stage, a puppy wants to be with you, so capitalise on this and keep practising the verbal cue, and rewarding your puppy with a treat and lots of praise when he comes to you.

Now you are ready to introduce some distractions. Try calling him when someone else is in the garden, or wait a few minutes until he is investigating a really interesting scent.

When he responds, make a really big fuss of him and give him extra treats so he knows it is worth his while to come to you. If your puppy responds, immediately reward him with a treat.

If he is slow to come, run away a few steps and then call again, making yourself sound really exciting. Jump up and down, open your arms wide to welcome him; it doesn't matter how silly you look, he needs to see you as the most fun person in the world.

When you have a reliable recall in the garden, you can venture into the outside world. Do not be too ambitious to begin with; try a recall in a quiet place with the minimum of distractions so you can be more certain of success.

Do not make the mistake of only asking your dog to come at the end of his allotted exercise period. What is the incentive in coming back to you if all you do is clip on his lead, marking the end of his free time?

Instead, call your dog at random times, giving him a treat and a stroke, and then letting him go free again. In this way, coming to you – and focusing on you – is always rewarding.

Stationary exercises

The Sit and Down are easy to teach, and mastering these exercises will be rewarding for both you and your Weimaraner. The Weimaraner can be exuberant, so it is useful if you have a means of bringing proceedings to a standstill before everyone gets carried away!

Sit

The best method is to lure your Weimaraner into position, and for this you can use a treat or his food bowl.

Hold the reward (a treat or food bowl) above his head. As he looks up, he will lower his hindquarters and go into a sit. Practise this a few times and when your puppy understands what you are asking, introduce the verbal cue, "sit".

When your Weimaraner understands the exercise, he will respond to the verbal cue alone, and you will not need to reward him every time he sits.

However, it is a good idea to give him a treat on a random basis when he co-operates as this will keep him guessing!

Down

This is an important lesson, and can be a lifesaver if an emergency arises and you need to bring your Weimaraner to an instant halt.

You can start with your dog in a sit or a stand for this exercise. Stand or kneel in front of him and show him you have a treat in your hand. Hold the treat just in front of his nose and slowly lower it towards the ground, between his front legs.

As your Weimaraner follows the treat he will go down on his front legs and, in a few moments, his hindquarters will follow. Close your hand over the treat so he doesn't cheat and get the treat before he is in the correct position. As soon as he is in the down, give him the treat and lots of praise.

Keep practising, and when your Weimaraner understands what you want, introduce the verbal cue, "down".

Control exercises

These exercises are not the most exciting, but they are important in establishing a relationship of mutual respect with your Weimaraner.

Wait

This exercise teaches your Weimaraner to wait in position until you give the next command; it differs from the stay exercise where he must stay where you have left him for a more prolonged period.

The most useful application of wait is when you are getting your dog out of the car and you need him to stay in position until you clip on his lead.

Start with your puppy on the lead to give you a greater chance of success. Ask him to sit, and stand in front him.

Step back one pace, holding your hand, palm flat, facing him. Wait a second and then come back to

stand in front of him. You can then reward him and release him with a word, such as "OK" .

Practise this a few times, waiting a little longer before you reward him, and then introduce the verbal cue, "wait".

You can reinforce the lesson by using it in different situations, such as asking your Weimaraner to "wait" before you put his food bowl down.

Stay

You need to differentiate this exercise from the wait by using a different hand signal and a different verbal cue.

Start with your Weimaraner in the down as he is most likely to be secure in this position. Stand by his side and then step forwards, with your hand held back, palm facing the dog.

Step back, release him, and then reward him. Practise until your Weimaraner understands the exercise and then introduce the verbal cue, "stay".

Gradually increase the distance you can leave your puppy, and increase the challenge by walking around him – and even stepping over him – so that he learns he must stay until you release him.

Leave

A response to this verbal cue means that your Weimaraner will learn to give up a toy on request, and it follows on that he will give up anything when he is asked, which is very useful if he has got hold of a forbidden object.

This is very important for the Weimaraner who has a tendency to become possessive over things he values.

It is not simply a matter of obeying the verbal cue to "leave"; it is establishing the status quo in which you are the decision-maker and your Weimaraner is ready to co-operate with you.

Self-control is a very important lesson for the exuberant Weimaraner.

The leave command can be taught quite easily when you are first playing with your puppy. As you gently take a toy from his mouth, introduce the verbal cue, "leave", and then praise him.

If he is reluctant, swap the toy for another toy or a treat. This will usually do the trick.

Do not try to pull the toy from his mouth if he refuses to give it up, as you will make the situation confrontational.

The Weimaraner has a stubborn streak and he does not give in easily. The best strategy is to let the toy go dead in your hand, and then swap it for a new toy, or a really high-value treat, so this becomes the better option.

Remember to make a big fuss of your Weimaramer when he does as you ask. Being in your good books means a lot to a Weimaraner so never stint on giving him verbal praise and telling him he is the best dog in the world.

Facing page: Be creative in your training and avoid confrontation.

Opportunities for Weimaraners

The versatile Weimaraner was bred to be the perfect all-rounder in his role as a working gundog; he has a flexible mind and thrives on mental stimulation. This is a breed who is prepared to take on any new challenge, and with positive, reward-based training, he will make his mark in any sport you care to try.

Good Citizen Scheme

The Kennel Club Good Citizen Scheme was introduced to promote responsible dog ownership, and to teach dogs basic good manners. In the US there is one test; in the UK there are four award levels: Puppy Foundation, Bronze, Silver and Gold.

Exercises within the scheme include:

- Walking on lead

- Road walking

- Control at door/gate

- Food manners

- Recall

- Stay

- Send to bed

- Emergency stop

Obedience

If your Weimaraner has mastered basic obedience, you may want to get involved in competitive obedience. The exercises include: heelwork at varying paces with dog and handler following a pattern decided by the judge, stays, recalls, retrieves, sendaways, scent discrimination and distance control.

The exercises get progressively harder as you progress up the classes. The Weimaraner will have no trouble learning these exercise but you need to be aware that this discipline calls for a very high degree of precision and accuracy which does not suit all dogs, or all handlers.

Rally O

If you do not want to get involved in the rigours of Competitive Obedience, you may find that a sport called Rally O is more to your liking. This is loosely based on Obedience, and also has a few exercises borrowed from agility when you get to the highest levels. Handler and dog must complete a course, in the designated order, which has a variety of different exercises that could number from 12 to 20. The course is timed and the team must complete within the time limit that is set, but there are no bonus marks for speed.

The great advantage of Rally O is that it is very relaxed, and anyone can compete. Indeed, it has proved very popular for handlers with disabilities as they are able to work their dogs to a high standard and compete on equal terms with other competitors.

Flyball

This is a fast and furious sport, which is always accompanied by a huge amount of enthusiastic barking.

It is a team sport where four dogs are selected to run in a relay race against an opposing team. The dogs are sent out by their handlers to jump four hurdles, catch the ball from the flyball box and then return over the hurdles. The teams compete against the clock, and a heat is decided when the fourth dog crosses the finishing line.

The Weimaraner is a natural retriever, and if this instinct is encouraged early on with lots of play and reward, he will soon become ball obsessed, which is the key to a great flyball dog.

Agility is a great choice for the athletic Weimaraner.

Agility

This is a demanding sport, which is a perfect match for the Weimaraner with his quick mind and athletic physique.

In Agility, the dog completes an obstacle course, which includes jumps, tunnels, weaving poles and contact equipment (A-frame, dog-walk and seesaw) under the guidance of his owner. You need a good element of control, as the dog completes the course off the lead.

In competition, each dog completes the course individually and is assessed on both time and accuracy. The dog that completes the course with the fewest faults, in the fastest time, wins the class.

Field trials

These are highly competitive, sometimes arduous events, which are staged to replicate a day's shooting in the field.

A well-trained Weimaraner can excel in these competitions where dogs are marked for their ability to carry out the skills they were bred for, working with a variety of game.

As an HPR (hunt, point retrieve) breed, the Weimaraner is tested on his ability to quarter the ground in search of quarry, to point game, to flush on command and to retrieve tenderly to hand either from land or from water.

Tracking

The Weimaraner has an excellent nose and is a natural choice for this demanding sport where the dog must learn to follow scent trails of varying age, over different types of terrain. In the UK tracking is incorporated into Working Trials where a dog must compete in two other elements (control and agility) but in the US it is a sport in its own right.

Showing

Exhibiting a dog in the show ring sounds easy but, in fact, it entails a lot of training and preparation.

Your Weimaraner will have to be calm and confident in the busy show atmosphere, so you need to work on his socialisation, and also take him to ringcraft classes so you both learn what is required in the ring.

Your Weimaraner will be subjected to a detailed 'hands on' examination by the judge; he must learn to stand still in a show pose and to move on a loose lead so the judge can assess his gait.

Showing at the top level is highly addictive, so watch out – once you start, you will never have a free date in your diary!

Dancing with dogs

This is a relatively new discipline and is growing in popularity, despite the hard work that is involved.

Dog and handler perform a choreographed routine to music, allowing the dog to show off an array of tricks and moves, which delight the crowd.

There are two categories: heelwork to music where heelwork in different positions makes up the larger percentage of the routine, and canine freestyle which allow the dog to work at a greater distance from the handler, and will include some of the more spectacular moves.

Both categories demand a huge amount of training but if you keep sessions light-hearted, with plenty of tasty food rewards on offer, the Weimaraner will prove to be a real crowd-pleaser!

Health care

We are fortunate that the Weimaraner is a healthy breed and with good routine care, a well-balanced diet, and sufficient exercise, most will experience few health problems.

However, it is your responsibility to put a programme of preventative health care in place, and this should start from the moment your puppy, or older dog, arrives in his new home.

Vaccinations

Dogs are subject to a number of contagious diseases. In the old days, these were killers, and resulted in heartbreak for many owners. Vaccinations have now been developed, and the occurrence of the major infectious diseases is now very rare.

However, this will only remain the case if owners of pet dogs adhere to a strict policy of vaccinating their dogs.

There are vaccinations available for the following diseases:

Adenovirus (Canine Adenovirus): This attacks the liver and affected dogs have a classic 'blue eye'.

Distemper: A viral disease which causes chest and gastro-intestinal damage. The brain may also be affected, leading to fits and paralysis.

Parvovirus: Causes severe gastro enteritis, and most commonly affects puppies.

Leptospirosis: This bacterial disease is carried by rats and affects many mammals, including humans. It causes liver and kidney damage.

Rabies: A virus that affects the nervous system and is invariably fatal. The first signs are abnormal behaviour when the infected dog may bite another animal or a person. Paralysis and death follow. Vaccination is compulsory in most countries. In the UK, dogs travelling overseas must be vaccinated.

Kennel cough: There are several strains of kennel cough, but they all result in a harsh, dry, cough. This disease is rarely fatal; in fact most dogs make a good recovery within a matter of weeks and show few signs of ill health while they are affected.

However, kennel cough is highly infectious among dogs that live together so, for this reason, most boarding kennels will insist that your dog is protected by the vaccine, which is given as nose drops.

Lyme disease: This is a bacterial disease transmitted by ticks. The first signs are limping, but the heart, kidneys and nervous system can also be affected.

The ticks that transmit the disease occur in specific regions, such as the north-east states of the USA, some of the southern states, California and the upper Mississippi region. Lyme disease is still rare in the UK so vaccinations are not routinely offered.

Vaccination programme

In the USA, the American Animal Hospital Association advises vaccination for core diseases, which they list as distemper, adenovirus, parvovirus and rabies. The requirement for vaccinating for non-core diseases – leptospriosis, lyme disease and kennel cough – should be assessed depending on a dog's individual risk and his likely exposure to the disease.

In the UK, vaccinations are routinely given for distemper, adenovirus, leptospirosis and parvovirus.

In most cases, a puppy will start his vaccinations at around eight weeks of age, with the second part given a fortnight later. However, this does vary depending on the individual policy of veterinary practices, and the incidence of disease in your area.

You should also talk to your vet about whether to give annual booster vaccinations.

This depends on an individual dog's levels of immunity, and how long a particular vaccine remains effective.

Parasites

No matter how well you look after your Weimaraner, you will have to accept that parasites (internal and external) are ever present, and you need to take preventative action.

Internal parasites: As the name suggests, these parasites live inside your dog. Most will find a home in the digestive tract, but there is also a parasite that lives in the heart. If infestation is unchecked, a dog's health will be severely jeopardised, but routine preventative treatment is simple and effective.

External parasites: These parasites live on your dog's body – in his skin and fur, and sometimes in his ears.

Roundworm

This is found in the small intestine, and signs of infestation will be a poor coat, a pot belly, diarrhoea and lethargy. Pregnant mothers should be treated, but it is almost inevitable that parasites will be passed on to the puppies.

For this reason, a breeder will start a worming programme, which you will need to continue. Ask your vet for advice on treatment, which will be ongoing throughout your dog's life.

Tapeworm

Infection occurs when fleas and lice are ingested; the adult worm takes up residence in the small intestine, releasing mobile segments (which contain eggs) that can be seen in a dog's faeces as small rice-like grains.

The only other obvious sign of infestation is irritation of the anus. Again, routine preventative treatment is required throughout your Weimaraner's life.

Heartworm

This parasite is transmitted by mosquitoes, and so will only occur where these insects thrive. A warm environment is needed for the parasite to develop, so it is more likely to be present in areas with a warm, humid climate.

However, it is found in all parts of the USA, although its prevalence does vary. At present, heartworm is rarely seen in the UK.

Heartworm live in the right side of the heart. Larvae can grow up to 14 inches (35.5cm) in length. A dog with heartworm is at severe risk from heart failure, so preventative treatment, as advised by your vet, is essential. Dogs living in the USA should have regular blood tests to check for the presence of infection.

Lungworm

Lungworm, or Angiostrongylus vasorum, is a parasite that lives in the heart and major blood vessels supplying the lungs. It can cause many problems, such as breathing difficulties, blood-clotting problems, sickness and diarrhoea, seizures, and can be fatal.

The parasite is carried by slugs and snails, and the dog becomes infected when ingesting these, often accidentally when rummaging through undergrowth. Lungworm is not common, but it is on the increase and a responsible owner should be aware of it.

Fortunately, it is easily preventable and even affected dogs usually make a full recovery if treated early enough. Your vet will be able to advise you on the risks in your area and what form of treatment may be required.

Fleas

A dog may carry dog fleas, cat fleas, and even human fleas. The flea stays on the dog only long enough to have a blood meal and to breed, but its presence will result in itching and scratching.

If your dog has an allergy to fleas, which is usually a reaction to the flea's saliva, he will scratch himself until he is raw.

Preventative treatment needs be administered on a routine basis; this can be in the form of a tablet, spot-on treatment, an insecticidal spray or shampoo. Ask your vet for advice on what product to use.

Bear in mind that the whole environment your dog lives in will need to be sprayed, and all other pets living in your home will also need to be treated.

How to detect fleas

You may suspect your dog has fleas, but how can you be sure? There are two methods to try.

Run a fine comb through your dog's coat, and see if you can detect the presence of fleas on the skin, or clinging to the comb. Alternatively, sit your dog on white paper and rub his back. This will dislodge faeces from the fleas, which will be visible as small brown specks. To double check, shake the specks on to damp cotton-wool. Flea faeces consists of the dried blood taken from the host, so if the specks turn a lighter shade of red, you know your dog has fleas.

Ticks

These are blood-sucking parasites which are most frequently found in rural areas where sheep or deer are present. The main danger is their ability to pass lyme disease to both dogs and humans. Lyme disease is prevalent in some areas of the USA, although it is still rare in the UK. The treatment you give your dog for fleas generally works for ticks, but you should discuss the best product to use with your vet.

How to remove a tick

If you spot a tick on your dog, do not try to pluck it off as you risk leaving the hard mouth parts embedded in his skin. The best way to remove a tick is to use a fine pair of tweezers, or you can buy a tick remover. Grasp the tick head firmly and then pull the tick straight out from the skin. If you are using a tick remover, check the instructions, as some recommend a circular twist when pulling. When you have removed the tick, clean the area with mild soap and water.

Ear mites

These parasites live in the outer ear canal. The signs of infestation are a brown, waxy discharge, and your dog will continually shake his head and scratch his ear. If you suspect your Weimaraner has ear mites, a visit to the vet will be needed so that medicated ear drops can be prescribed.

Fur mites

These small, white parasites are visible to the naked eye and are often referred to as 'walking dandruff'. They cause a scurfy coat and mild itchiness. However, they are zoonetic – transferable to humans – so prompt treatment with an insecticide prescribed by your vet is essential.

Harvest mites

These are picked up from the undergrowth, and can be seen as a bright orange patch on the webbing between the toes, although this can be found elsewhere on the body, such as on the ear flaps. Treatment is effective with the appropriate insecticide.

Skin mites

There are two types of parasite that burrow into a dog's skin. *Demodex canis* is transferred from a mother to her pups while they are feeding. Treatment is with a topical preparation, and sometimes antibiotics are needed.

The other skin mite, *Sarcoptes scabiei*, causes intense itching and hair loss. It is highly contagious, so all dogs in a household will need to be treated, and this will involve repeated bathing bathing with a medicated shampoo.

Common ailments

As with all living animals, dogs can be affected by a variety of ailments. Most can be treated effectively after consulting with your vet, who will prescribe appropriate medication and will advise you on how to care for your dog's needs.

Here are some of the more common problems that could affect your Weimaraner, with advice on how to deal with them.

Anal glands

These are two small sacs on either side of the anus, which produce a dark-brown secretion that dogs use when they mark their territory. The anal glands should empty every time a dog defecates but if they become blocked or impacted, a dog will experience increasing discomfort. He may nibble at his rear end,

or scoot his bottom along the ground to relieve the
irritation. Treatment involves a trip to the vet, who
will empty the glands manually. It is important to do
this without delay or infection may occur.

Dental problems

Good dental hygiene will do much to minimise
gum infection and tooth decay, which is why teeth
cleaning should be part of your regular care routine.
If tartar accumulates to the extent that you cannot
remove it by brushing, the vet will need to intervene.
In a situation such as this, an anaesthetic will need
to be administered so the tartar can be removed
manually.

Diarrhoea

There are many reasons why a dog has diarrhoea,
but most commonly it is the result of scavenging, a
sudden change of diet, or an adverse reaction to a
particular type of food.

If your dog is suffering from diarrhoea, the first step
is to withdraw food for a day. It is important that he
does not dehydrate, so make sure that fresh drinking
water is available. However, drinking too much can
increase the diarrhoea, which may be accompanied
by vomiting, so you will need to limit.

After allowing the stomach to rest, feed a bland diet, such as white fish or chicken with boiled rice, for a few days. In most cases, your dog's motions will return to normal and you can resume usual feeding, although this should be done gradually.

However, if this fails to work and the diarrhoea persists for more than a few days, you should consult you vet. Your dog may have an infection which needs to be treated with antibiotics, or the diarrhoea may indicate some other problem which needs expert diagnosis.

Ear infections

The Weimaraner has drop ears which means that air does not circulate freely, potentially creating an ideal environment for infection. A healthy ear is clean with no sign of redness or inflammation, and no evidence of a waxy brown discharge or a foul odour. If you see your dog scratching his ear, shaking his head, or holding one ear at an odd angle, you will need to consult your vet.

The most likely causes are ear mites, an infection, or there may be a foreign body, such as a grass seed, trapped in the ear. Depending on the cause, treatment is with medicated ear drops, possibly containing antibiotics. If a foreign body is suspected, the vet will need to carry out further investigations.

The ear leathers are fine, and can be caught when a Weimaraner is running through undergrowth, causing profuse bleeding.

This is not serious but it is advisable to keep an antiseptic in your first-aid box so you can clean the wound throughly.

Eye problems

The Weimaraner has medium-sized eyes, set well apart, which are neither sunken nor prominent. This lack of exaggeration means that a Weimaraner's eyes should not be predisposed to infection or vulnerable to injury or trauma, which is the case with breeds such as the Pekingese, that have somewhat bulging eyes.

However, if your Weimaraner's eyes look red and sore, he may be suffering from conjunctivitis. This may, or may not, be accompanied with a watery or a crusty discharge.

Conjunctivitis can be caused by a bacterial or viral infection, it could be the result of an injury, or it could be an adverse reaction to pollen.

You will need to consult your vet for a correct diagnosis, but in the case of an infection, treatment with medicated eye drops is effective.

Foreign bodies

In the home, puppies – and some older dogs – cannot resist chewing anything that looks interesting. The toys you choose for your dog should be suitably robust to withstand damage, but children's toys can be irresistible.

Some dogs will chew – and swallow – anything from socks, tights, and any other items from the laundry basket to golf balls and stones from the garden. Obviously, these items are indigestible and could cause an obstruction in your dog's intestine, which is potentially lethal.

The signs to look for are vomiting, and a tucked up posture. The dog will often be restless and will look as though he is in pain. In this situation, you must get your dog to the vet without delay, as surgery may be needed to remove the obstruction.

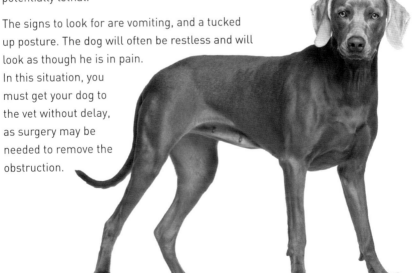

Heatstroke

As a working gundog, the Weimaraner needed an efficient respiratory system and, as a result, he is not prone to over-heating as is the case with breeds, such as the Bulldog or the Boxer, that have short muzzles and up-turned noses. However, all dogs can be affected by heatstroke – and temperatures do not need to be extreme for this to occur.

If the weather is warm, make sure your Weimaraner has access to shady areas, and wait for a cooler part of the day before going for a walk. Be extra careful if you leave your Weimaraner in the car as the temperature can rise dramatically – even on a cloudy day. Heatstroke can happen very rapidly, and unless you are able to lower your dog's temperature, it can be fatal.

If your dog appears to be suffering from heatstroke, lie him flat and work at lowering his temperature by spraying him with cool water and covering him with wet towels. As soon as he has made some recovery, take him to the vet, where cold intravenous fluids can be administered.

Lameness/limping

There are a wide variety of reasons why a dog can go lame, from a simple muscle strain, to a fracture, ligament damage, or more complex problems with the joints. If you are concerned about your dog, do not delay in seeking help.

As your Weimaraner becomes more elderly, he may suffer from arthritis, which you will see as general stiffness, particularly when he gets up after resting.

It will help if you ensure his bed is in a warm draught-free location, and if your Weimaraner gets wet after exercise, you must dry him thoroughly. If he seems to be in pain, consult your vet who will be able to help with pain relief medication.

Skin problems

If your dog is scratching or nibbling at his skin, first check he is free from fleas. There are other external parasites which cause itching and hair loss, but you will need a vet to help you find the culprit.

An allergic reaction is another major cause of skin problems. It can be quite an undertaking to find the cause of the allergy, and you will need to follow your vet's advice, which often requires eliminating specific ingredients from the diet, as well as looking at environmental factors.

Breed-
specific
disorders

Like all pedigree dogs, the Weimaraner does have some breed-related disorders. If diagnosed with any of the diseases listed here, it is important to remember that they can affect offspring so breeding from such dogs should be discouraged.

There are now recognised screening tests to enable breeders to check for affected individuals and hence reduce the prevalence of these diseases within the breed. DNA testing is also becoming more widely available, and as research into the different genetic diseases progresses, the number of DNA tests is increasing.

Atopic dermatitis

This skin disorder is found in dogs with an inherited disposition to inflammatory and itching skin disease. It usually becomes evident within the first couple of years and may progress to a secondary bacterial infection or fungal infections may develop.

It is the result of low immunity to allergens in the environment.

Eye disorders

Cataract

Cataracts are an opacification of the lens that tends to occur in older dogs. There are varying degrees of severity, with the inherited form often having little effect on eyesight but, if necessary, surgery is usually a successful treatment.

Screening is available for this condition.

Entropion

This is an inherited eye condition which presents as an in-rolling of the eyelids. This ranges in severity from mild to the more serious, where surgical correction is required because of the pain and damage that is inflicted on the eyeball.

Hypothyroidism

This condition, caused by an under-active thyroid gland, is not uncommon in the breed. This gland produces a hormone called thyroxine and low levels in the body produce symptoms which include: lethargy, cold intolerance, lack of appetite or constant hunger.

Other breeds suffering from this condition become obese and develop a thinning coat, but this is not the case with Weimaraners so it is important to be aware of the other signs to aid diagnosis. Treatment is with hormone replacement therapy.

Joint disorders

Hip dysplasia

This is a malformation of the hip joint where the head of the femur does not align with the cup of the hip socket. Resulting lameness ranges from mild to severe. Surgery can be effective.

All potential breeding stock should be x-rayed and hip-scored.

Patellar luxation

This condition, which involves a slipping kneecap, is usually detected when a dog puts in the occasional skip or 'bunny hop' when he is moving. No treatment is needed in mild cases but surgery may be required if the condition is severe.

Syringomyelia

This is relatively rare but it has been reported in the breed. The condition is the result of a malformation of the hind brain fluid-filled cavities which are located in the spinal cord of the upper neck.

An affected dog may have a bunny hopping gait and experience pain in the shoulder area. MRI screening will be needed for a correct diagnosis.

Unfortunately, there is no effective treatment; breeding should be avoided from suspect animals.

Wobbler disease

This is caused by an abnormality of the neck vertebrae causing rear leg ataxia, which is seen as a wobbling walk. This may deteriorate to such an extent that the dog suffers total paralysis of the hindquarters.

Summing up

It may give the pet owner cause for concern to find out about health problems that may affect their dog. But it is important to bear in mind that acquiring some basic knowledge is an asset, as it will allow you to spot signs of trouble at an early stage. Early diagnosis is very often the means to the most effective treatment.

Fortunately, the Weimaraner is a generally healthy and disease-free dog, with his only visits to the vet being annual check-ups.

In most cases, owners can look forward to enjoying many happy years with this affectionate and highly entertaining companion.

Useful addresses

Breed & Kennel Clubs
Please contact your Kennel Club to obtain contact information about breed clubs in your area.

UK
The Kennel Club (UK)
1 Clarges Street London, W1J 8AB
Telephone: 0870 606 6750
Fax: 0207 518 1058
Web: www.thekennelclub.org.uk

USA
American Kennel Club (AKC)
5580 Centerview Drive, Raleigh, NC 27606.
Telephone: 919 233 9767
Fax: 919 233 3627
Email: info@akc.org
Web: www.akc.org

United Kennel Club (UKC)
100 E Kilgore Rd, Kalamazoo,
MI 49002-5584, USA.
Tel: 269 343 9020
Fax: 269 343 7037
Web:www.ukcdogs.com

Australia
Australian National Kennel Council (ANKC)
The Australian National Kennel Council is the administrative body for pure breed canine affairs in Australia. It does not, however, deal directly with dog exhibitors, breeders or judges. For information pertaining to breeders, clubs or shows, please contact the relevant State or Territory Body.

International
Fédération Cynologique Internationalé (FCI)
Place Albert 1er, 13, B-6530 Thuin, Belgium.
Tel: +32 71 59.12.38
Fax: +32 71 59.22.29
Web: www.fci.be

Training and behavior
UK
Association of Pet Dog Trainers
Telephone: 01285 810811
Web: www.apdt.co.uk

Canine Behaviour
Association of Pet Behaviour Counsellors
Telephone: 01386 751151
Web: www.apbc.org.uk/

USA
Association of Pet Dog Trainers
Tel: 1 800 738 3647
Web: www.apdt.com

American College of Veterinary Behaviorists
Web: www.dacvb.org

American Veterinary Society of Animal Behavior
Web: www.avsabonline.org

Australia
APDT Australia Inc
Web: www.apdt.com.au

For details of regional behaviorists, contact the relevant State or Territory Controlling Body.

Activities
UK
Agility Club
www.agilityclub.co.uk

British Flyball Association
Telephone: 01628 829623
Web: www.flyball.org.uk

USA
North American Dog Agility Council
Web: www.nadac.com

North American Flyball Association, Inc.
Tel/Fax: 800 318 6312
Web: www.flyball.org

Australia
Agility Dog Association of Australia
Tel: 0423 138 914
Web: www.adaa.com.au

NADAC Australia
Web: www.nadacaustralia.com
Australian Flyball Association
Tel: 0407 337 939
Web: www.flyball.org.au

International
World Canine Freestyle Organisation
Tel: (718) 332-8336
Web: www.worldcaninefreestyle.org

Health
UK
British Small Animal Veterinary Association
Tel: 01452 726700
Web: www.bsava.com

Royal College of Veterinary Surgeons
Tel: 0207 222 2001
Web: www.rcvs.org.uk

Alternative Veterinary Medicine Centre
Tel: 01367 710324
Web: www.alternativevet.org

USA
American Veterinary Medical Association
Tel: 800 248 2862
Web: www.avma.org

American College of Veterinary Surgeons
Tel: 301 916 0200
Toll Free: 877 217 2287
Web: www.acvs.org

Canine Eye Registration Foundation
The Veterinary Medical DataBases
1717 Philo Rd, PO Box 3007,
Urbana, IL 61803-3007
Tel: 217-693-4800
Fax: 217-693-4801
Web: www.vmdb.org

Orthopaedic Foundation of Animals
2300 E Nifong Boulevard
Columbia, Missouri, 65201-3806
Tel: 573 442-0418
Fax: 573 875-5073
Web: www.offa.org

American Holistic Veterinary Medical
Association
Tel: 410 569 0795
Web: www.ahvma.org

Australia
Australian Small Animal Veterinary
Association
Tel: 02 9431 5090
Web: www.asava.com.au

Australian Veterinary Association
Tel: 02 9431 5000
Web: www.ava.com.au

Australian College Veterinary Scientists
Tel: 07 3423 2016
Web: www.acvsc.org.au

Australian Holistic Vets
Web: www.ahv.com.au